BARRON'S BOOK NOTES

CHARLES DICKENS'S

Hard Times

BARRON'S BOOK NOTES

CHARLES DICKENS'S

Hard Times

BY

Michael Adams

SERIES COORDINATOR
Murray Bromberg
Principal, Wang High School of Queens
Holliswood, New York

Past President
High School Principals Association of New York City

BARRON'S EDUCATIONAL SERIES, INC.

ACKNOWLEDGMENTS

Our thanks to Milton Katz and Julius Liebb for their advisory
assistance on the *Book Notes* series.

8 6 8 5 7

All inquiries should be addressed to:
Barron's Educational Series, Inc.
113 Crossways Park Drive
Woodbury, New York 11797

Library of Congress Catalog Card No. 85-4071

International Standard Book No. 0-8120-3518-6

Library of Congress Cataloging in Publication Data

Adams, Michael
  Charles Dickens's Hard times.

  (Barron's book notes)
  Bibliography: p. 118
  Summary: A guide to reading "Hard Times" with a
critical and appreciative mind encouraging analysis of
plot, style, form, and structure. Also includes background
on the author's life and times, sample tests, term paper
suggestions and a reading list.
  1. Dickens, Charles, 1812–1870. Hard times.
[1. Dickens, Charles. Hard times. 2. English literature—
History and criticism] I. Title. II. Series.
PR4561.A75 1985   823'.8   85-4071
ISBN 0-8120-3518-6

PRINTED IN THE UNITED STATES OF AMERICA

567   550   98765432

CONTENTS

ADVISORY BOARD

HOW TO USE THIS BOOK

You have to know how to approach literature in order to get the most out of it. This *Barron's Book Notes* volume follows a plan based on methods used by some of the best students to read a work of literature.

Begin with the guide's section on the author's life and times. As you read, try to form a clear picture of the author's personality, circumstances, and motives for writing the work. This background usually will make it easier for you to hear the author's tone of voice, and follow where the author is heading.

Then go over the rest of the introductory material—such sections as those on the plot, characters, setting, themes, and style of the work. Underline, or write down in your notebook, particular things to watch for, such as contrasts between characters and repeated literary devices. At this point, you may want to develop a system of symbols to use in marking your text as you read. (Of course, you should only mark up a book you own, not one that belongs to another person or a school.) Perhaps you will want to use a different letter for each character's name, a different number for each major theme of the book, a different color for each important symbol or literary device. Be prepared to mark up the pages of your book as you read. Put your marks in the margins so you can find them again easily.

Now comes the moment you've been waiting for—the time to start reading the work of literature. You may want to put aside your *Barron's Book Notes* volume until you've read the work all the way through. Or you may want to alternate, reading the *Book Notes* analysis of each section as soon as you have finished reading the corresponding part of the original. Before you move on, reread crucial passages you don't fully understand. (Don't take this guide's analysis for granted—make up your own mind as to what the work means.)

Once you've finished the whole work of literature, you may want to review it right away, so you can firm up your ideas about what it means. You may want to leaf through the book concentrating on passages you marked in reference to one character or one theme. This is also a good time to reread the *Book Notes* introductory material, which pulls together insights on specific topics.

When it comes time to prepare for a test or to write a paper, you'll already have formed ideas about the work. You'll be able to go back through it, refreshing your memory as to the author's exact words and perspective, so that you can support your opinions with evidence drawn straight from the work. Patterns will emerge, and ideas will fall into place; your essay question or term paper will almost write itself. Give yourself a dry run with one of the sample tests in the guide. These tests present both multiple-choice and essay questions. An accompanying section gives answers to the multiple-choice questions as well as suggestions for writing the essays. If you have to select a term paper topic, you may choose one from the list of suggestions in this book. This guide also provides you with a reading list, to help you when you start research for a term paper, and a selection of provocative comments by critics, to spark your thinking before you write.

THE AUTHOR AND HIS TIMES

In 1839, Charles Dickens, whose popular novel *Oliver Twist* had just been published, took a trip to Manchester, a city in northwest England. It was a trip that was to change his life and result in one of his most bitter and controversial novels, *Hard Times*.

In Manchester, Dickens was taken to see cotton mills typical of those that had sprung up in northern England as a result of the Industrial Revolution. The invention of the steam engine in the late eighteenth century was a major force behind this "revolution." Power became accessible and inexpensive, and factories boomed with production.

There was a darker side to this teeming productivity, however. The methods of organizing the workers for maximum efficiency often led to miserable working conditions; long hours, hard work, dangerous machinery. Young children were often put to work, despite laws that were meant to prevent the abuse of minors. Workers were housed in slums with filthy sanitation. Factories poured poisonous smoke into the atmosphere, darkening the skies and threatening the health of anyone who lived in the town.

Laws were passed that offered some protection to these workers, but factory owners often disregarded them, and the laws were difficult to enforce. So the dangerous machinery and poor sanitation continued, and many owners felt they had no responsibility to their employees except to pay them wages that were established by the laws of supply and demand. Prosperity, so said many in charge, depended on high profits and inexpensive labor.

The basis for much of this abuse, according to writers such as Dickens and the Scots essayist and historian Thomas Carlyle (to whom *Hard Times* is dedicated), was the political philosophy of Utilitarianism. Utilitarianism had its roots in the laissez-faire doctrine of the Scots economist Adam Smith, expressed in his book *The Wealth of Nations* (1776). Laissez-faire means, in the original French, "leave alone," and Smith's book detailed his opposition to governmental interference in the economy of a nation.

Smith's ideas were elaborated by the English philosopher Jeremy Bentham, the founder of Utilitarianism, and then further developed by the English economist and philosopher John Stuart Mill. In simple terms, the Utilitarians sought "the greatest happiness for the greatest number"—in other words, whatever was correct for the majority, particularly in regard to economic profit, was thought to be correct for everyone. The Utilitarians brought about important social reforms.

Yet, as Dickens and others pointed out, Utilitarianism was subject to abuse, particularly where the poor minority were concerned. In striving for greater profits that would benefit the nation, management often exploited the workers, and politicians winked at their exploitation. In *Hard Times*, Gradgrind Sr. is portrayed as a strict Utilitarian, who practices his philosophy at home and in the school he governs. Like others of his kind, he sees little reality beyond profit and loss.

After visiting Manchester, Dickens wrote to a friend: "I went to Manchester and saw the worst cotton mill. And then I saw the best . . . There was no great difference between them." The workers made a lasting impression on Dickens. He wrote: ". . . what I have seen has disgusted me and astonished me beyond all measure. I mean to strike the heaviest blow in my power for these unfortunate creatures."

For Dickens, striking the "heaviest blow" meant using his pen. Few writers have ever been so popular in their lifetimes. His work combines elements of hilarious and thrilling entertainment with sharp condemnations of society, and many readers believe he blended these elements more skillfully than any other novelist in the English language—before or since.

Born in Portsmouth, England, in 1812, he was the son of John Dickens, a clerk for the Navy. The elder Dickens, who later moved his family to London, was known as a warm-hearted, generous man, who, however, often found himself broke. (In the novel *David Copperfield,* Dickens offers a fictionalized portrait of John Dickens in the character of the lovable but irresponsible Mr. Micawber.)

John Dickens's free-spending ways resulted in two traumatic incidents for young Charles. At the age of twelve, when his family's finances slipped badly, Dickens was forced to work in a blacking factory (which manufactured boot blacking or shoe polish). Dickens was devastated! He felt abandoned and discarded by his family. The lofty ambitions to become a man of learning crumbled. Throughout his life he refused to discuss the experience with anyone but vowed he would never again have to endure such hardship. His wife and children never knew until after his death that he had worked in a factory as a child.

The terror and anger this incident caused found its way into several of Dickens's novels as he created many children orphaned or abandoned by their parents: Jo in *Bleak House*, David Copperfield, Oliver Twist, Nicholas Nickleby and his sister Kate, Sissy Jupe in *Hard Times*, and others. While some accuse Dickens of often sentimentalizing these characters, others point to how those young people reflect the deep sense of rejection he must have felt.

The second traumatic incident occurred soon after Dickens left the blacking factory, when his father was arrested for debt and sent to prison. For three months Mrs. Dickens and her children lived there with him, allowed their freedom during the day, but locked in at night. Charles lived elsewhere, hating the confines of the prison and embittered at the complicated laws that kept his father there. Little by little, Charles Dickens was developing the soul of a reformer. Life in a debtor's prison became the basis for one of his more complex and mature novels, *Little Dorrit*.

A change in his father's fortunes allowed Charles to return to school. He had always been precocious, reading hungrily whatever he could—newspapers, history, fairy tales, all of which influenced his later writing. A love of the theater inspired him to create lively characters, suspense, comic high spirits, and excitement in his work.

After leaving school, Dickens worked for a time as an office boy in a law firm, and then as a newspaper reporter, writing general news for one paper, reporting on the affairs of Parliament for another. It was through these jobs that Dickens developed a lifelong distrust of the law, a contempt that emerged in such novels as *Bleak House* and *Hard Times.*

He began to write short fictional sketches about London life and characters, using the pen name "Boz." The broad appeal of these sketches led one editor to ask Dickens to try an experiment—to write a novel in serial form, several chapters per month. Novels were usually published in three volumes, making them expensive for the average person. Publishing them in a monthly magazine would make them more accessible and inexpensive.

The result was *The Pickwick Papers* (1836–37), an immediate success. It may be difficult to understand how the weekly installments of a book could create the fever pitch of excitement that *Pickwick* did. But if you remember that, without television or movies, Victorians turned to books for their entertainment, you might understand that they awaited the next installment just as eagerly as you may look forward to a new episode of your favorite television show. "Boz" was the toast of London, and everyone wanted to know who he was.

Dickens soon dropped his pen name as he continued to write serials, sometimes beginning one at the same time he was writing another. And while *Pickwick Papers* is a comic romp through the towns and countryside of England, the later novels began to explore some of the murkier aspects of big city life in the nineteenth century. *Oliver Twist* (1837–38) examines the plight of the poor who lurked in London's underworld. *Nicholas Nickleby* (1838–39) deals in part with the abuses of schools that mistreated and victimized their students. *Bleak House* (1852–53) looks at the weighty and impossibly complicated affairs of the court system.

Yet if Dickens had been nothing more than a

moralizing social critic, it's unlikely that his works would be read and enjoyed today. He was, first and foremost, one of the supreme entertainers in literary history. His books have intricate plots, memorable characters, brilliant comedy, intense emotion. But Dickens, despite his popularity, was constantly afraid of losing his public. If the sale of a magazine that contained one of his serials began to drop, Dickens might alter the plot in some way to bring people back. That he was able to combine popular appeal with literary genius (second only to Shakespeare, according to many) is a testament to his incredible skill.

Unfortunately, Dickens's personal life did not always match the success of his writing career. At the time he was writing *The Pickwick Papers* (1836) he married Catherine Hogarth, the daughter of one of his editors. For a time the marriage was quite happy, and Catherine eventually bore him ten children. But as the years passed, Dickens began to find his wife lazy, clumsy, socially inept—not at all the kind of wife he felt a man of his stature deserved.

There are those who feel that Dickens so idealized Catherine's sister Mary (whose death at seventeen devastated Dickens) that no one could hope to compare with her. This worship of the ideal woman can be seen in many of Dickens's female characters: Agnes Wickfield in *David Copperfield*, Esther in *Bleak House*, Little Nell in *The Old Curiosity Shop*, Kate Nickleby in *Nicholas Nickleby*, Sissy Jupe in *Hard Times*, and others. Some readers feel that this need to put certain women on a pedestal prevented his female characters from attaining the depth and complexity of their male counterparts.

Dickens's vanity grew with his success, and he began more and more to see Catherine critically. The couple began to separate, first emotionally, and then literally. You'll see in *Hard Times* how his frustration at the divorce laws found its way into that novel.

Dickens began to see a young actress, Ellen Ternan, who at eighteen was young enough to be his daughter. He loved her deeply, and she was at his side when he died.

Dickens's writing skills and his social conscience merged when he began a weekly periodical in 1850. He invited many of his friends to contribute history, fiction, reviews, and essays that portrayed social matters. The purpose of the periodical was "to cherish the light of Fancy which is inherent in the human heart." (Remember this phrase as you read *Hard Times*.)

Each issue (or number) of the magazine, called *Household Words*, dealt with a social problem: government aid for education, alcoholism, illiteracy, factory accidents, industrial schools. These articles often championed radical ideas, and they were so skillfully blended with entertainment that the magazine was an enormous success. Pioneers in sanitary and housing reform gave Dickens much credit for bringing their causes to the general public.

It was at a time when sales of *Household Words* were low that Dickens decided to write a weekly serial that would match the popularity of some of his earlier works. Since his previous novels had been written in monthly numbers, the task of writing weekly episodes was exhausting. Yet he was spurred by the challenge of writing about the horrors of the Industrial Revolution that had so shocked him in Manchester fifteen years before. In this way *Hard Times* was born and helped the magazine's popularity considerably. Dickens said at the time that the purpose of the novel was not to create social unrest, but to foster understanding between management and labor.

Hard Times has not enjoyed the critical success of such Dickens's masterpieces as *David Copperfield* (1849–50) and *Great Expectations* (1860–61). Some readers have charged that it does not explore factory life with the same perceptive detail with which he exposed the courts in *Bleak House*. (And it is strange that, for all of the talk of worker hardship in *Hard Times*, Dickens never takes us within the factories themselves.) Some readers even point to the Stephen Blackpool sequences as melodramatic and unbelievable.

The novel does have its champions; some regard *Hard Times* as one of his finest works of satire. They cite its economy (it is one of Dickens's shortest novels), its passion, and its prophetic portrait of social ills in their praise of the book. As always, Dickens tells a wonderful story, one with suspense, humor, deeply felt emotion, and tenderness. Dickens the entertainer is never blotted out by Dickens the reformer.

How successful was *Hard Times* as a document of radical social change? It's often impossible to gauge the exact influence a book has on a culture, since its effects materialize slowly. And Dickens was not the only writer pointing to the hideous results of industrialization. (Elizabeth Gaskell, another novelist and a friend of Dickens, wrote about similar topics in such books as *North and South*.)

Yet his immense readership guaranteed that the public would become aware of the plight of the factory workers in greater numbers than could be reached by any newspaper.

By the 1890s, conditions for the workers had improved somewhat, thanks largely to the workers themselves, who formed trade unions that forced reforms on employers. Even though Dickens criticizes the unions in *Hard Times*, he would have been the first to applaud these reforms. Such passionate social critics as George Bernard Shaw acclaimed Dickens as a supreme influence on the betterment of English society. (He thought Dickens's novel *Little Dorrit* was as radical and rebellious a work as Karl Marx's *Das Kapital*.)

In 1858, Dickens began to give a series of public readings from his own work. He was a marvelous performer, as popular onstage as he was in print. But the exhausting performances damaged his health, which declined seriously over the next few years.

Despite illness he took a trip to America. He had been there years before, and a resulting book, *American Notes* (1842), made some Americans furious at the way Dickens had portrayed them. But during this visit in 1867, he was greeted with a frenzy we might reserve for a rock star today.

Dickens returned to England in extremely poor health. He died of a paralytic stroke on June 9, 1870. At the time, he was writing *The Mystery of Edwin Drood*, which he never finished.

Even if you've never read a Dickens novel, it's likely that you know his work anyway. Countless movies, television shows, musicals, and plays have been based on his work. Scarcely a Christmas season goes by without a new version of *A Christmas Carol* (1843). So you may "know" Dickens without having read a word of his writing. But there's no substitute for his own words. No adaptation can do justice to his genius. Like all great writers, Dickens created worlds both recognizable and magical. Like Shakespeare, Dickens embraced all levels of society and invested each one with his own generous touch of humanity.

THE NOVEL

The Plot

Coketown is a grimy, smelly industrial town in northern England, its houses and skies blackened by smoke from factory chimneys. One of its leading citizens is Thomas Gradgrind, future member of Parliament and governor of the local school. Gradgrind lives with his wife and five children, including the eldest, Louisa, and Tom, Jr.

When we first see Gradgrind, he is observing a typical class in his school, taught by Mr. M'Choakumchild. Gradgrind lectures the teacher on the school's philosophy: "Facts" are important, nothing else but facts. All else is "fancy"—sentiment, imagination. Cecilia Jupe ("Sissy"), the daughter of an acrobatic rider and clown with a traveling troupe of performers, is asked to define a horse. She can't, but Bitzer, an ambitious student, can. His answer is based entirely on fact.

Gradgrind later spies Louisa and young Tom outside the horse-riding (circus) tent, trying to catch a glimpse of the performers. Shocked at their interest in such frivolity, Gradgrind seeks the advice of his friend, Josiah Bounderby, a banker and factory owner. They conclude that it must be Sissy Jupe's influence that is responsible. They try to find her father, but discover that he's deserted Sissy to prevent her from seeing him lose his talents. Gradgrind offers to take care of Sissy by bringing her into his household, hoping that Louisa will see what happens to someone who was raised on fancy, not fact. Sissy accepts his invitation.

Bounderby objects to the arrangement. He has dragged himself up from poverty to a position of power and wealth. Treating the "lower classes" with such kindness is a mistake to him; these people are spoiled enough. Bounderby lives with his housekeeper, Mrs. Sparsit, a member of the faded aristocracy. She has lost her money, but not her disdain for those she considers beneath her.

Another resident of Coketown is Stephen Blackpool, a factory worker.

Once happily married, Stephen is separated from his wife, a drunkard who wanders off for months at a time, only to return to shame him. Stephen is in love with Rachel, another worker, but the two of them can't marry because of divorce laws that favor the wealthy. For Stephen and Rachel, life is a "muddle."

Gradgrind is elected to Parliament. It is decided that his son Tom should work at Bounderby's bank and that his daughter Louisa should marry Bounderby. Louisa tries to communicate to her father that the marriage would be a mistake, but Gradgrind refuses to hear of anything that speaks of love or sentiment. Only Sissy, who discontinues her education because she is thought "unteachable," but who stays on in the Gradgrind household, understands Louisa's plight. But Louisa is too proud to accept Sissy's compassion. When the wedding takes place, only Tom Gradgrind is truly happy, thinking his life at the Bounderby bank will be much easier with his sister around to defend him.

A year after the wedding, changes have taken place in Coketown. Mrs. Sparsit now lives in an apartment at the bank, where the sneaky Bitzer has become the messenger. And a new person has come to town—James Harthouse, an aristocratic young man recruited by Gradgrind's political party.

Harthouse is immediately attracted to Louisa, and he accurately senses that the Bounderby marriage is not a success. He makes plans to alleviate his own boredom by trying to win Louisa's affections.

Meanwhile, the workers of Coketown are attempting to form a union to protect their rights. They are led by Slackbridge, a power-hungry union organizer. Stephen refuses to join the union because he's convinced it won't help their plight, and because of a promise he's made to Rachael. True to their pact, the workers shun Stephen, who eventually loses his job when loyalty to his co-workers prevents him from denouncing them to Bounderby.

Stephen is forced to leave town to look for work. Louisa offers him money, which he refuses, but Tom has something else in mind. He asks Stephen to linger for several evenings around the bank, which Stephen innocently does. After waiting for three evenings, nothing happens, so Stephen sets off from Coketown.

The relationship between Harthouse and Louisa begins to intensify. Their every move is watched by Mrs. Sparsit, eager to prove the fact of adultery and to see the Bounderby marriage crumble.

Soon after Stephen's departure, it's learned that the bank has been robbed. Since Stephen was seen lingering outside the bank, he is implicated in the crime. So is Mrs. Pegler, a woman Stephen befriended, who comes to Coketown every year to watch Bounderby from afar. Louisa immediately suspects that Tom is responsible for the robbery, but he denies it.

Mrs. Sparsit believes that Harthouse and Louisa

are about to elope. As Mrs. Sparsit sees Louisa board a train, she follows her, only to lose her along the way. But Louisa is not on her way to meet Harthouse. She is going to her father's home, and there she confesses to him that Harthouse is waiting to run away with her. She begs for her father's advice. Faced with the failure of his "facts-only" philosophy, Gradgrind is shattered. He offers Louisa shelter.

Sissy, now an important part of the Gradgrind household, goes to Harthouse on her own to persuade him to leave town. He is powerless in the face of Sissy's moral goodness, and he agrees to leave Louisa and Coketown behind.

The robbery still remains unsolved. Mrs. Sparsit is triumphant when she discovers Mrs. Pegler, but the old woman turns out to be Bounderby's mother, who had supposedly deserted him at an early age. Bounderby is revealed as a fraud and a liar, but he is unrepentant.

The search for Stephen continues. Rachael can't understand why he has not responded to her letter asking him to return. But the mystery is solved when Sissy and Rachael take a quiet walk in the country. They discover that Stephen has fallen into an abandoned mine and is near death. When he is brought from the pit, he is reunited briefly with Rachael before he dies.

Knowing that Stephen's death will point the finger of guilt at him, Tom runs away, on Sissy's advice, to Sleary's circus. When Louisa, Sissy, and Gradgrind find him there, he is playing a silly clown in one of the circus acts. He feels no guilt for what he has done, and Gradgrind again must face a failed product of his philosophy.

Despite Bitzer's attempts to arrest Tom, Sleary helps the young culprit escape to a port where he can sail to safety. Sleary offers the final parting words of wisdom: people need amusement as much as they need work.

The characters go on to their respective futures. Mrs. Sparsit will live unhappily with her relative, Lady Scadgers. Bounderby will die of a fit. A repentant Tom will die before he has a chance to return home. Gradgrind will grow old, alienated from those who once shared his philosophy. Rachael will continue to live in town, occasionally helping a drunken wretch of a woman who shows up from time to time. Sissy will marry and have children, but there is no such reward in store for Louisa. She must be content with helping those less fortunate than she. Nothing changes for the workers of Coketown. They continue to be exploited from every side, all of life still "a muddle."

The Characters
MAJOR CHARACTERS
Thomas Gradgrind, Sr.

A leading businessman of Coketown and governor of the school, Gradgrind becomes a member of Parliament during the course of the story. He is married and the father of five, including Louisa and Tom, Jr., two of the major characters.

Gradgrind is a strict disciple of the philosophy of Utilitarianism that prizes hard fact above all else. Anything not a fact is considered "fancy" or sentiment. Gradgrind practices what he preaches—to the letter. Not only are his learning techniques taught in the school he governs, but his children have been raised by its laws. Their learning has been strictly scientific, free from the "corrupting" influence of poetry, fairy tale, or song.

The novel charts Gradgrind's growing realization that his theories, when applied without the humane influence of the heart, can be destructive. A marriage arranged for profit and convenience between Louisa and Bounderby ends in disaster. Tom, Jr., becomes a liar and a thief, forced to escape the law in disguise.

A basically decent man (unlike Bounderby), Gradgrind is not beyond redemption, according to Dickens. Largely through the influence of Sissy Jupe and the trauma of Louisa's failed marriage, Gradgrind grows in wisdom and experience. He pays for his earlier insensitivity by seeing the harmful results of his philosophy: Tom's life of crime, Bitzer's cold-hearted practicality, and Louisa's emotional breakdown. By the end of the novel, however, he is a wiser and better man.

Louisa Gradgrind (Mrs. Bounderby)

Daughter of Thomas Gradgrind and, later, wife to Josiah Bounderby, Louisa is first seen curiously peeking at the goings-on at the horse-riding performance. Her action is symbolic of her yearning to experience more than the hard scientific facts she has learned all her life. Instinctively seeking romance and laughter when all she has known are theory and statistics, Louisa is viewed by Dickens as a pathetic product of her father's philosophy.

Attractive and sensitive, Louisa has always masked her emotions under a cool and passive facade. She is often linked symbolically to fire: Dying embers represent her fading hopes for happiness, and the fires of Coketown chimneys that are frequently hidden beneath smoke represent her inward passions.

Her humanity emerges gradually as the novel progresses. At first she cares only for her brother Tom; for his sake she marries Bounderby, a much older man. But as the lovelessness of her marriage takes its toll, she reaches out, first to Stephen Blackpool, an oppressed factory worker, and then to James Harthouse, an arrogant aristocrat who tries to seduce her. Pressed to the brink of madness by the temptation that Harthouse offers, Louisa throws herself on her father's mercy. Nothing in her previous education has prepared her to handle her emerging passions. She saves herself from disgrace just in time, helped by the friendship of Sissy Jupe, who represents the wisdom of the heart—a wisdom Louisa has never known.

Louisa and Gradgrind's changes of character mark the greatest progression in the novel. Louisa begins as a passive, daydreaming girl and ends as a mature, generous, and humane young woman. She dedicates her life to helping those less fortunate than she.

Josiah Bounderby

A powerful citizen of Coketown, Bounderby owns a factory and a bank. If Gradgrind represents the Utilitarian philosophy in the novel, Bounderby symbolizes the greedy capitalist, shockingly insensitive to the needs of workers.

Bounderby (whose name is British slang for "cad") is also the "Bully of humility," a self-made man who endlessly repeats the story of his rise from poverty and childhood abuse to his current position of power. He claims to loathe the trappings of wealth—a grand home, beautiful furnishings, art objects—but he nonetheless collects them avidly.

His greatest source of pride is Mrs. Sparsit, his housekeeper, a woman of high station brought low by a bad early marriage. The delicious irony that this highborn lady should now work for him—who was born a pauper—is irresistible to Bounderby. He reminds everyone, including Mrs. Sparsit, of this striking contrast time and again.

Bounderby is shattered by his marriage to Louisa, who never respects him as he thinks he deserves He is also highly embarrassed when it is discovered that Mrs. Pegler is his mother and that he has paid her to stay out of his life. He suffers a dual humiliation when Louisa deserts him and Mrs. Pegler reveals that he has lied about his past. To make matters worse, he learns that Mrs. Sparsit— the one person whose respect for him seemed unshakable—has long held him in contempt.

Bounderby is a one-dimensional character. He learns nothing from his trials, and he seems to have no inner life. He begins and ends as a blustering, opinionated fool. Drawn from a comic tradition that Dickens began with *The Pickwick Papers*, Bounderby is "flat," almost a cartoon. His effect on other characters in the book, such as Stephen Blackpool and Louisa, is powerful and real, but he is not as fully rendered a character as his friend Gradgrind.

Cecilia Jupe ("Sissy")

Daughter of a horse-riding acrobat and clown at Sleary's traveling circus, Sissy is taken into the

Gradgrind household when her father deserts her. From the first, Sissy is treated by Gradgrind and Bounderby as a bad influence on the Gradgrind children, one who has been poorly educated and corrupted by the vulgar show folk who raised her. But Sissy symbolizes the "Wisdom of the Heart" that has been sadly lacking among the Gradgrinds. Little by little, her positive influence is felt. Louisa's sister Jane is visibly happier than Louisa ever was as a child, and even the self-pitying Mrs. Gradgrind wonders, as she lays dying, what has been missing from their lives.

When Louisa leaves her husband and returns to her childhood home, Sissy becomes a dominant force in the novel. She offers Louisa the healing balm of friendship to bring her from the brink of emotional breakdown. Sissy confronts Harthouse with her ultimatum that he leave Coketown. She comforts Rachael and helps find Stephen. And she provides Tom with a means of escape via Sleary's circus. Sissy, more than any other character, proves to Gradgrind that the wisdom of the heart is no myth, but is as real as any fact he ever learned.

Sissy is awarded the Victorian ideal of true happiness—a husband and children. Although never sure her father still lives, she painstakingly keeps the jar of nine-oils to soothe his bruises should he ever return.

Stephen Blackpool

A forty-year-old factory worker, Stephen Blackpool is honest, hardworking, and kind. He symbolizes all the oppressed workers of the town as he toils long hours for little pay and lives in impoverished conditions. But Stephen is also burdened by circumstances that greatly add to his misery. His wife became a drunkard and a public disgrace some years ago. She returns from time to time, tattered and dirty, in spite of his having paid her to stay away. The divorce laws prevent Stephen from ridding himself of her and marrying his true love, Rachael. Even though passing thoughts sometimes tempt Stephen to kill his wife, he knows in his heart there is nothing he can do to improve his desperate situation.

Stephen also refuses to join the workers' union on principle, a decision that causes him to be shunned by his fellow workers and ultimately fired. After having left town to find work, he is on his way back to Coketown to clear himself of a false accusation of crime when he falls into the shaft of an abandoned mine. His subsequent death makes him a helpless victim of a social system that abuses and exploits the working man.

While Stephen Blackpool's surname suggests the waters clouded by industrial waste, his first name suggests St. Stephen, the first Christian martyr. Some readers see Stephen as a pathetic, even tragic figure. Others regard him as an obvious symbol, too contrived to be a successful fictional creation. As you read you'll have to come to your own assessment of him. Whatever opinion is held of Stephen, it is generally agreed that his catchphrase for the confused unhappiness of life—"It's a muddle"—is one of the novel's most memorable lines.

Mrs. Sparsit

Once a lady of wealth, Mrs. Sparsit was brought low when her young husband wasted a fortune and died, leaving her penniless. Known for her Coriolanian (Roman style) nose and dark eyebrows, she is first seen as Mr. Bounderby's house-keeper and then as his tenant in rooms at the bank. She and Bounderby enjoy a symbiotic relationship: he needs her to give him impressive credentials, and she needs him to remind the world of her lofty past.

When Bounderby marries Louisa, Mrs. Sparsit is forced to watch the world go by from her window, but frequent visits to the Bounderby home provide her with plenty of opportunity to practice her busybody ways. She frequently reminds Bounderby of Louisa's weaknesses as a wife and begins an organized and obsessive effort to prove that Louisa and Harthouse are about to run away together. All the while, she praises Bounderby to his face and calls him a "noodle" behind his back.

Eager to prove herself correct about Louisa, Mrs. Sparsit is shattered by Louisa's decision to return to the Gradgrind home. And she is reduced to embarrassment and misery when she unwittingly is instrumental in revealing Bounderby as a liar and a fraud. Her relationship with Bounderby ends with hostility and ill-bred name-calling.

Mrs. Sparsit (the "sparse" of her name suggesting the scantiness or meagerness of her character) represents the faded aristocracy so hated by Dickens for its laziness, smugness, and disregard for those less fortunate.

Thomas Gradgrind, Jr. (Tom)

Tom represents another dismal product of the Gradgrind philosophy of education. From the very first he is selfish, self-centered, and insensitive. He sees his sister's disastrous marriage to Bounderby as a means for an easier life for himself, with little regard to what such a match might mean to Louisa. Tom is also easily swayed by the trappings of Harthouse's wealth, and it is his willingness to talk freely to Harthouse about Louisa that clears the path for the older man to try to seduce her. Even worse, Tom shows no guilt about robbing the bank to pay his gambling debts and then implicating Stephen Blackpool, an innocent man. Tom's actions indirectly lead to Stephen's death. But Tom is unrepentant; he even resents Louisa for telling the truth. Dickens characterizes him as a hypocrite and a monster.

James Harthouse

An aristocrat who comes to Coketown to enter politics for Gradgrind's Hard Fact party, Harthouse represents the jaded upper classes. Cynical and amoral, Harthouse sets out to seduce Louisa, motivated not by love or passion, but out of boredom. One philosophy is as good as the next as far as he's concerned, and his lack of commitment has driven him from one lackluster career to the next. He is not a villain in the sense that he sets out to do evil, but he is harmful nonetheless, like the drifting iceberg that wrecks ships. His only nod to goodness comes when he faces Sissy and decides to leave town at her request. His name ("hearthouse") is an ironic comment on his lack of compassion.

Some have felt that Harthouse is a believable character. Others argue that he is just a plot contrivance. How do you feel? What evidence can you offer in support of your opinion?

MINOR CHARACTERS

Bitzer

You first see Bitzer in M'Choakumchild's classroom, offering the perfect factual definition of a horse. The direct opposite of Sissy Jupe, he is the perfect product of the Gradgrind philosophy—emotionless, coldhearted, and ambitious. Bitzer later becomes a porter at Bounderby's bank, spies for Mrs. Sparsit, and nearly catches Tom Gradgrind before his escape. Everything about him is so light—hair, complexion, eyes—that he is colorless. What does such a description tell you? If someone suggested that Bitzer was pale because he had been drained of the colors of humanity, would you agree or disagree?

Rachael

A factory worker who is Stephen's best friend, Rachael is selfless, loving, patient, and long-suffering. Her name reminds us of the Biblical Rachel, whom Jacob loved but had to wait many years before he could marry. Like her Biblical counterpart, Rachael is in love with a man she can't marry, and she accepts her fate. She compassionately helps the wretched Mrs. Blackpool whenever that lady wanders into town, drunk and abusive. Rachael continues her care of the woman after Stephen's death.

Mrs. Pegler

Mrs. Pegler is Bounderby's mother, paid by him to stay out of his life. This sweet old woman is content to visit Coketown once a year and gaze at her successful son from a distance. For a time she is implicated in the robbery because she has been seen with Stephen, but her "capture" by Mrs. Sparsit only reveals the lies Bounderby has been telling about his "cruel" childhood.

Mr. Sleary

Owner of Sleary's Horse-riding, a traveling circus, Sleary is kindhearted and generous. He speaks with a lisp (the result of chronic asthma) and represents a philosophy—"People must be amused"—that is the direct opposite of Gradgrindism. He is responsible for helping Tom escape from Bitzer's clutches to safe passage overseas.

Mr. M'Choakumchild

A teacher at Gradgrind's model school, M'Choakumchild is a recent graduate of an educational "factory." There he learned a wide variety of subjects but little about the art of teaching beyond stuffing the heads of his students with facts. He represents some of the worst abuses of the educational system.

Mrs. Blackpool

Mrs. Blackpool, Stephen Blackpool's wife, turned to drink some years ago and sold their possessions to support her habit. Stephen paid her to stay away, but she returns on drunken jags, to bring shame and disgrace on her husband, as well as prolonged emotional anguish.

Slackbridge

Slackbridge is the union organizer who urges the workers to reject Stephen for refusing to join their ranks. An unattractive and sour man, Slackbridge represents those who would exploit the workers to satisfy their own need for power.

Mr. Jupe
A horse-riding acrobat, and Sissy's father, Jupe never appears in the book, but his presence is felt through Sissy's devotion to him. He deserts Sissy rather than have her see him lose his agility. Jupe is assumed dead when his dog Merrylegs returns alone to Sleary's circus.

Do you see Jupe's desertion of his daughter as an act of kindness or an act of cruelty?

Childers and Kidderminster
Childers and Kidderminster are performers in Sleary's circus, who deflate Bounderby's pomposity early in the book.

Other Elements

SETTING

The action of *Hard Times* takes place in the city of Coketown and the surrounding countryside Coketown represents a number of industrial towns in northern England—such as Manchester and Preston. It was Dickens's visit to Manchester almost fifteen years before he wrote *Hard Times* that gave him the impetus to write the novel. For further research as he was beginning to write his novel, Dickens traveled to the mill town of Preston, scene of a famous labor strike in 1853. Although Dickens did not choose to dramatize a strike in *Hard Times*, he probably found the model for the union organizer Slackbridge in Preston.

The atmosphere of Coketown is essential to the novel's mood. Dickens's images suggest an urban jungle. "Serpents" of smoke rise from factory chimneys to clog the skies with soot. The steam engine has an "elephant's head" that monotonously lifts up and down and fills the air with horrible sounds. All the red brick buildings are blackened with soot, and each building looks tediously like the next. Even on a sunny day, the sun can't penetrate the grime in the air. From a distance the town looks like a blur of smoke and dirt.

The depressing surroundings take their toll on the citizens, who are consistently woeful. The dreariness of the town is symbolically linked to the philosophies that govern the citizens' lives. No sunlight can penetrate the clouds, and no sense of imagination or fun is allowed to alleviate the tedium of the workaday world.

The main characters are no less affected by their surroundings. Louisa and Tom are so deprived of color and fun in their lives that the arrival of a traveling circus is a source of guilty pleasure for them. Stephen Blackpool and Rachael are first seen together in the midst of a grimy rain. Coketown offers them no other pleasure but their friendship. Gradgrind, Bounderby, Mrs. Sparsit, and Bitzer are all humorless, unhappy people. Their grim personalities are as much products of their environment as they themselves are victims of the philosophies that rule their lives.

Some readers have pointed to minor inaccuracies in Dickens's portrayal of Coketown. Not all such towns had these unsanitary conditions or unspeakable working situations. But Dickens was working for a *poetic* reality, not the literal truth.

His occasional exaggerations or inventions are done to prove a point, and few can deny that he achieves a remarkable portrait of an industrial city whose suffocating influence is never far from your mind as you read. In fact, "Coketown" has come to represent a term for such grimy towns throughout the world, some of which still exist, although laws for pollution control have done a great deal to lessen their hazardous effects.

THEMES

Hard Times is a unified, compact novel. Its themes often overlap as Dickens points an accusing finger at a specific time and place: England during the time of the Industrial Revolution. The themes are discussed throughout The Story section as they relate to the plot. They are listed here so that you may be aware of them as you read.

Major Themes
1. THE WISDOM OF THE HEART VS. THE WISDOM OF THE HEAD
Gradgrind represents the wisdom of the head. His philosophy is based on utilitarianism, which seeks to promote "the greatest happiness for the greatest number." The philosophy is based on scientific laws that dictate that nothing else is important but profit, and that profit is achieved by the pursuit of cold, hard facts. Everything that isn't factual is considered "fancy," or imagination.

The wisdom of the heart is embodied in Sissy Jupe. Simple, considered uneducable, Sissy brings goodness and purity to bear on many of the characters, including Gradgrind. As he sees the products of his philosophy shattered around him, particularly Louisa and Tom, he begins to wonder if the wisdom of the heart that others have talked about really exists. Sissy proves to him that it does, and she salvages a great deal that might have been lost.

Closely related to this theme is man's need for "amusement." Sleary, the owner of the traveling circus, insists that people can't work and learn all the time—an idea once odious to Gradgrind.

2. EXPLOITATION OF THE WORKING CLASS

We see this theme worked out through the character of Stephen Blackpool, a factory worker. Stephen's life is "a muddle," in part because he and the other workers are exploited from all sides. Their employer, Bounderby, thinks that their lives are easy and that their complaints stem from selfishness and greed. The utilitarians who run the schools and the government are interested only in profit. The union organizers are driven by power-hungry self-interest. At one point Stephen indicates that the workers have bad leaders because only bad leaders are offered to them. Throughout the novel, the workers are almost all faceless, nameless individuals. They are called by the reductive term "hands," because it is their working hands that are important to the employers—not their souls or brains or spirits.

3. THE EFFECTS OF THE INDUSTRIAL REVOLUTION

Closely connected with the theme of exploitation, this theme is more all-encompassing. It reveals the abuses of a profit-hungry society that result in a variety of social disgraces: poor education for its children; smoke-filled cities and polluted water; dangerous factory machines; dreadful working conditions; substandard housing for the workers. This corrupt society is more interested in productivity and profit than in the health and happiness of its citizens. These issues are still relevant today in different degrees in different parts of the world; well over a century has passed since Dickens the reformer wrote *Hard Times*, but some of the abuses to which he called attention still linger.

4. THE FAILURE OF THE UTILITARIAN EDUCATION

The opening scene in M'Choakumchild's classroom sets the tone for this theme. Students are taught according to what is factual and are ordered to avoid anything imaginative. As governor of the school, Gradgrind not only sets the policy of hard facts but also practices it in the raising of his own five children. Educators like Gradgrind see children as "empty vessels" to be filled to the brim with facts and statistics. They never take into account the child's need for poetry, song, and fiction—those elements that feed the heart and soul, as well as the mind. The failure of this system is seen through Louisa and Tom Gradgrind, and the ambitious sneak Bitzer.

5. THE ARROGANCE OF THE UPPER CLASSES

Mrs. Sparsit and James Harthouse represent this theme. Mrs. Sparsit clings fiercely to her heritage and faded glamor. She is haughty to those "beneath" her and despises the efforts of the workers to organize a union.

Harthouse is revealed as cynical and direction-less. He treats his seduction of Louisa as a diversion, without thinking of the consequences of his actions.

A related minor theme is the worship of the upper classes by those of the middle class. This is demonstrated in Bounderby's pride over Mrs. Sparsit's lofty background, in his acquisition of the trappings of wealth (despite his apparent disdain for them), and in Tom's admiration for Harthouse's worldly ways.

Minor Themes

LOYALTY: Examples of loyalty (and its absence) are seen throughout the novel. Sissy remains loyal to her father and his memory, even though he deserted her. Rachael and Stephen are loyal to one another over the years despite their inability to be married. They both remain loyal to Mrs. Blackpool—he by enduring her presence, and Rachael by caring for her—when she comes to town. The most touching example of loyalty is Merrylegs, Jupe's dog, who leaves his master only after the old man is dead.

Those who prove to have no sense of loyalty include Tom, who turns away from Louisa, his devoted sister; Bounderby, who shuns his mother; Stephen's fellow workers, who reject him when he won't join the union; and Bitzer, who turns against his mentor, Gradgrind.

PARENT AND CHILD: Portraits of parents and their children figure significantly in *Hard Times*. Only Sissy and her father are seen in a positive light.

All the others reveal mistreatment or indifference: Gradgrind and his brood; Bounderby and Mrs. Pegler; and Bitzer, who sends his mother to a workhouse.

IMPRISONMENT: The theme of imprisonment works both literally and symbolically. The workers of Coketown are imprisoned by their jobs and their lives, since they have no other place to go to find work. Stephen is trapped in this way, but also by the bonds of marriage, which for him are tightly wound. Gradgrind and Bounderby are imprisoned by their respective philosophies. Louisa is a prisoner of her father's educational principles. And all the characters are shackled by a society that cares less for them than it does for the "well-being" of the economy. Only Sissy, who follows the Golden Rule, seems free from these bonds, and it is she alone who "escapes" to happiness by the novel's end.

STYLE

Dickens's distinctive style is one of the most admired in the English language. Here are some of its notable characteristics, followed by examples from *Hard Times*.

1. USE OF WORDS AND SENTENCE STRUCTURE

Dickens had a great love of language, which reveals itself in elaborate descriptions of people, places, and events. Long, complex sentences are common, but the words are rarely wasted. When simplicity is called for, Dickens can be frugal with

his words. If he does get carried away, remember
that his readers were used to long, spacious books
with full descriptions. Books provided the main
source of entertainment for Victorians, so readers
liked to get their money's worth!

Look at the second paragraph in Chapter 10, Book
the First. (It begins "In the hardest working part
of Coketown;"). The entire paragraph is one sentence, built of prepositional phrases and subordi-
nate clauses that lead to the introduction of Stephen Blackpool. Not only is this device highly
descriptive, but it underlines the importance of the
subject of the sentence—Stephen Blackpool—and
provides a very dramatic way to introduce him.

2. REPETITION

Repeating words and phrases within a sentence
or paragraph adds emphasis and musicality to
Dickens's prose (and makes it fun to read aloud).

Read carefully the second paragraph of Chapter
1 of Book the First, beginning "The scene was . . ."
Notice the repetition of such phrases as "The emphasis was helped" and such words as "square."
This technique is typical of Dickens's style, and is
often imitated.

3. SYMBOLISM AND METAPHOR

Hard Times is rich in symbolism, from Louisa's
identification with fire to Tom's depiction as a sad
clown in one of the final scenes. Metaphorically,
Coketown is described as a jungle, its smoke a
series of serpents, its steam engine an elephant's
head.

Other metaphors abound. Gradgrind's hair is a
"plantation of firs"; Mrs. Gradgrind is "a bundle
of shawls"; time is compared to machinery, with

"innumerable horse-power." Watch for Dickens's use of metaphors as you read. Draw up a list of your favorites.

4. ALLUSIONS
Dickens peppers his works with allusions to literature, mythology, the Bible, current events. Most of his readers would be familiar with these allusions, but some of them might be confusing to the modern reader. This guide will help you to understand the most important ones.

5. RHETORICAL DEVICES
Rhetorical devices are those which mirror techniques used in speech-making: exclamatory sentences, direct address to the audience (and to characters), questions. There are times when you might feel that Dickens is making a speech rather than writing a novel. "Ah, rather overdone, M'Choakumchild," he chides the teacher in Chapter 2, Book the First. "Where was the man, and why did he not come back?" he wonders about Stephen Blackpool in Chapter 5, Book the Third. "Dear reader!" he says in the final chapter. Many readers find these devices pretentious and inflated, but others find them energizing and vivid. How do you feel about them? Do they contribute to your enjoyment of the book?

6. COMIC RELIEF
There are few greater comic writers than Dickens. Some say he is a better writer when he is comic than when he is serious and sentimental. *Hard Times* can be a grim and bitter novel, but it is saved from being completely depressing by its comic moments (although there are fewer in this novel

than in most of Dickens's work). The tension is relieved by Sleary and his troupe, by Mrs. Sparsit (before she decides to undo Louisa), even by the pathetic Mrs. Gradgrind with her total lack of logic.

Look at Chapter 6, Book the First, "Sleary's Horsemanship." The tension is high because Gradgrind and Bounderby have come to scold Jupe for bringing up so poorly educated a daughter. But Jupe is missing, and everyone is afraid of Sissy's reaction. Dickens relieves the tension by the comic jousting among Bounderby, Childers, and Kidderminster. Bounderby doesn't realize he's being made fun of, but the ways in which the two performers deflate his pomposity enliven a gloomy scene.

The lack of humor in the Stephen Blackpool scenes is one reason some readers feel these parts of the book are less successful than others.

POINT OF VIEW

A great entertainer, Dickens was a storyteller of the highest degree, and in *Hard Times*—as in most of his novels—he weaves a wonderful story. Dickens himself is the narrator, observing his characters, commenting upon them, and talking directly to the reader. (You saw in the style section how these devices work to pull in the reader.) With few exceptions (the first-person *David Copperfield* is one), Dickens favors this third-person point-of-view in his novels.

Dickens as narrator is selectively omniscient. For example, you may go for a long time without knowing what Tom is thinking, but then—for a brief moment or two—you'll be allowed entrance into Tom's mind. This choice of when and how you may see into the minds of the characters gives the narrator a great deal of power over how he wants you to view the story.

The strength of this narrator also dictates how you are to feel about each character. There's no ambiguity for Dickens here. You are told that Bounderby is a "bully," Tom a "hypocrite." Dickens is firm in these judgments; you know from the start which characters engage his sympathies and which repel him. Thus the morals he draws from his characters are very clear, down to the last bit of advice he offers in the novel's final paragraph.

You may find yourself resisting Dickens's opinions now and then, since his narrative voice is so strong. You may not need to be told, for example, that Tom is a monster and a hypocrite; you'd rather form that opinion yourself. If so, you're not alone among those who resent such narrative intrusion. But even if you do disagree with Dickens's moments of moralizing, you're not likely to question the passion and sincerity with which he voices these thoughts.

FORM AND STRUCTURE

Hard Times is divided into three sections, or books, and each book is divided into three separate chapters. The structure of the book takes its shape from the titles of the books, all of which are drawn from farming images that have biblical connotations.

Book the First, "Sowing," shows us the seeds planted by the Gradgrind/Bounderby philosophy: Louisa, Tom, and Stephen Blackpool.

Book the Second, "Reaping," reveals the harvesting of these seeds: Louisa's unhappy marriage, Tom's selfishness and criminal ways, Stephen's rejection from Coketown.

The first two books recall the biblical passage, "Whatsoever a man soweth, that shall he also reap" (Galatians 6:7).

Book the Third, "Garnering," details the results of the harvest. The title of the book recalls the biblical character Ruth. Ruth followed her mother-in-law Naomi to Naomi's homeland. There Ruth was allowed to follow the harvesters in the cornfield and gather what they did not pick up. The owner of the fields, Boaz, was so moved by her sense of duty and hard work that he took her for his wife.

In *Hard Times*, the characters must "take home" the results of what has been reaped—that is, they must live with the circumstances of their mistakes. Louisa's marriage fails, Tom must escape from the country, and Stephen dies.

Hard Times was written as a weekly magazine serial in twenty parts. This accounts for the number of chapters that end in suspense or in minor climaxes. You might enjoy guessing where each weekly installment began and ended. If so, don't look at the chart that follows.

Here are how the chapters were divided into weekly "numbers."

Installment Number		*Chapters*
1	Book the First	I–III
2		IV–V
3		VI
4		VII–VIII
5		IX–X
6		XI–XII
7		XIII–XIV

The Story

BOOK THE FIRST

CHAPTER I

In a large, plain, whitewashed schoolroom, three men stand in front of a class of young students. One of the men explains to the teacher his philosophy of education. It is *facts* that are important, *facts* that these children must learn. He emphasizes his theory again and again. The man speaking is not identified, but he is serious and severe. Everything about him is dry, inflexible, "square"—all hard edges and uniformity.

This chapter is short but important, because it establishes immediately one of Dickens's major themes: the destructiveness of the wrong kind of education on innocent minds. You'll see a detailed picture of this educational system in Chapter II, but the essence of its philosophy is shown here. Even before any of the characters is introduced by name, you hear a speech in praise of facts. That Dickens disapproves of this theory can be guessed by his description of the grim man speaking.

CHAPTER II

NOTE: Education in nineteenth-century England was in disarray, especially in schools for the poor. Many people virtually abandoned students to schools (both day schools and boarding schools) where they were sometimes completely ignored and often mistreated. (Dickens portrayed such a school in his earlier novel, *Nicholas Nickleby*.) The opposite extreme is exposed in *Hard Times*. Readers have pointed out that this chapter exaggerates very little in its depiction of the strict teaching methods of schools in factory towns.

The speechmaker in the classroom is Thomas Gradgrind, "a man of realities" and the school's governor. As he quizzes the class, he calls upon a new girl, whom he identifies by her classroom number, twenty. Huge classrooms were common in such schools, with hundreds of students assigned to a handful of teachers. Numbers were assigned to the students to ensure order.

The girl's name is Sissy Jupe, but Gradgrind insists on using her formal name, Cecilia. When Sissy tells him that her father works with the "horse-riding" (a traveling circus), Gradgrind won't hear of such a thing. If Jupe works with horses, Gradgrind insists, he must be a veterinarian.

Gradgrind's view of reality is so strict that he won't accept anything outside its realm. Not only won't he accept the use of the girl's nickname, but he changes Mr. Jupe's occupation to one less involved with "fancy"! Thomas Gradgrind is a major character in the novel, and you see here an early example of his inflexibility (as well as his refusal to face reality).

Gradgrind asks for a definition of a horse. Sissy is too shy to reply, but Bitzer, an eager student, is ready with the proper answer: "Quadruped. Graminivorous. Forty teeth, namely twenty-four grinders, four eye-teeth and twelve incisive. Sheds coat in the spring; in marshy countries, sheds hoofs, too. Hoofs hard, but requiring to be shod with iron. Age known by marks in mouth."

Does Bitzer's definition define a horse to your satisfaction? The facts are correct, but do the words suggest the beauty, the grace, the spirit of a horse? Dickens is just beginning to make his point that education requires more than the learning and memorizing of facts. These methods, according to Dickens, would prevent the student from learning things on their own or truly understanding what they had learned.

NOTE: For a portrait of a school that meets with Dickens's approval, see *David Copperfield*, where the hero attends a school run by Dr. Strong: "It was very gravely and decorously ordered," says David, "and on a sound system; with an appeal in everything, to the honour and good faith of the boys . . . We all felt we had a part in the management of the place, and in sustaining its character and dignity . . . We had noble games out of hours, and plenty of liberty." As you read this chapter in *Hard Times*, notice how the two schools contrast.

Sissy's shyness and Bitzer's aggressiveness are contrasted in this scene; their fates will intertwine in the novel. Notice the ray of sunlight that strikes both students. The sun brings out Sissy's natural, glowing colors, but it makes Bitzer appear pale and cold.

The third man in the room is a government officer, come to inspect the classroom. He questions the children, too. Would they wallpaper a room with pictures of horses or use a rug with flowers in its design? Those who answer yes are wrong. Horses don't walk on walls in real life, nor do people willingly walk on flowers. These decorations contradict fact. Any attempt by the students to talk about what they might "fancy"—or prefer—is stopped short by the government officer. The students must never fancy. They must stick to what is real.

The presence of the officer tells you that the school is government-run to teach the "lower classes." The man's disapproval of horse pictures and flowered carpets comes from an 1851 edict of a Department of Practical Art that recommended against such decorative touches!

The teacher of the class is Mr. M'Choakumchild, one of 140 teachers who have been produced by the same educational "factory." All of the teachers were formed in the same mold, all of their heads stuffed with facts.

tired lately—of everything. She shows no guilt or sorrow, despite her father's anger.

Gradgrind ends the discussion abruptly and orders his children to come home with him. On the way, he attempts to instill guilt in them by asking them what their friend Mr. Bounderby will think about their behavior. The mention of this name causes a distinct change in Louisa's emotions.

NOTE: Dickens compares Mr. Bounderby to Mrs. Grundy, a character in a popular English play, *Speed The Plough* (1798). Mrs. Grundy is often referred to (but never seen) in the play. She is a proper prudish neighbor, about whom the characters often say, "What will Mrs. Grundy think?" The character is still seen to represent a model of British propriety. You'll soon see why Dickens compares Bounderby to Mrs. Grundy.

CHAPTER IV

At Stone Lodge, Josiah Bounderby is talking to Mrs. Gradgrind. He is a rich, loud, balding balloon of a man, a "Bully of humility," and Gradgrind's best friend. Bounderby is telling Mrs. Gradgrind a story she has undoubtedly heard countless times before—the story of his early life. It's a tale of hardship and cruelty. Bounderby was deserted by his mother, raised by a wicked grandmother, and forced to support himself in a variety of odd jobs. The position he has achieved—and it's a lofty one, he'll be the first to tell you—is entirely due to his own perseverance.

NOTE: Dickens on education   In a speech given a few years after the novel was written, Dickens said: "I don't like that sort of school . . . where the bright childish imagination is utterly discouraged, and where those bright childish faces . . . are gloomily and grimly scared out of countenance; where I have never seen among the pupils, whether boys or girls, anything but little parrots and small calculating machines."

Dickens's disgust with the kind of education shown in the chapter is revealed in other ways:

1.   The title of the chapter, "Murdering the Innocents." It refers to an episode in the New Testament when King Herod, attempting to kill the Christ child, whose political power he feared, ordered all babies under the age of one year to be killed.

2.   The names of the characters. Dickens is celebrated for having fun with characters' names, and he often identifies the characters' inner lives by what he calls them. Look, for example, at the hard "gr" sound repeated in Gradgrind's name. The word "grind" also suggests (a) the way the man "grinds" his theories into students' heads and (b) an excessively diligent student.

As for M'Choakumchild, the implication of his name is all too clear! He's responsible for "choking" the children—with facts!

Is there evidence today of this kind of educational philosophy? Have you ever experienced anything similar to the way this school is run? Is there any benefit in this kind of strictness? Think about the kind of school you would operate as you read this chapter.

NOTE: M'Choakumchild's teaching methods are compared to Morgiana's in the story of Ali Baba in the *Arabian Nights*. Morgiana was Ali Baba's servant, who, in search of the forty thieves, looked into a large collection of jars. Discovering that all but one contained a thief, she boiled oil from the remaining jar and filled the others with the scalding liquid to kill the men inside. Dickens uses the allusion to scold M'Choakumchild. Beware! says Dickens. You may think you're only killing the imagination—the "fancy"—of these children, but instead you're harming them in more serious ways. As you will see, it's a warning that Gradgrind would do well to heed.

CHAPTER III

Gradgrind walks homeward from the school, which is in Coketown, an industrial city some distance from London. Coketown is a fictionalized representation of many industrial cities in northern England. "Coke" to coal miners is a residue coal product that can be used for fuel.

Gradgrind's home is on the outskirts of town. There he lives with a wife and five children, who have been raised, of course, according to fact. No nursery rhymes or fairy tales for them! His house, Stone Lodge, is as square and imposing as its owner.

As Gradgrind nears home, he passes by "Sleary's Horse-riding," where Sissy Jupe's father works.

Gradgrind notices with disapproval som circus's fanciful attractions.

NOTE: Dickens had great affection for th good-natured world of entertainment. He performers as overgrown children, fun-lo generous. The acts printed on the leafle grind sees are typical of those seen in fairs of the nineteenth century.

The circus is in full swing, with flags fl music blaring! Dickens contrasts the mu world of the circus with the plain, whit schoolroom for an obvious reason: fancy What evidence can you offer to show tha finds "fancy" more appealing?

Gradgrind is scornful of what he see scorn turns to shock when he spots two c children, Thomas and Louisa, among the peeking at the performers. How can it b that his children should be here at such place?

The chapter title is "A Loophole." A " refers on one level to the opening where trying to see the performance. Yet the means an escape or evasion from a contr regard the relationship between Gradgrin children as a contract—formal, busines binding—then their appearance at the c be the first sign of their eventual escape ber this as you read.

Louisa explains that she simply wan what the horse-riding was like, that she

NOTE: Bounderby is another of the novel's major characters. Our first clue to Dickens's opinion of him is in Bounderby's name: a "bounder" is British slang for an ill-bred, pushy person.

Dickens's description of Bounderby reveals one of the writer's famous stylistic traits—the repetition of words or phrases. In this paragraph he repeats the word "man" and phrases such as "a man who" and "a man with." The repetition creates a rhythm that accelerates and reaches a climax with the final line: "A man who was the Bully of humility." The "music" created by these rhythms is particularly Dickensian. Try reading this passage aloud (or similar passages) to appreciate the full flavor of Dickens's prose.

Gradgrind arrives home with Tom and Louisa. He immediately criticizes his wife for allowing them to leave their studies. The perpetually sickly Mrs. Gradgrind can only sigh and ineffectively scold her children.

Mrs. Gradgrind is both comic and pathetic in her attempts to raise her children by her husband's principles. She can do little more than parrot his orders when she tells them to "go and be somethingological directly," a reference to the vast number of subjects (whose titles end in "ology," or "the study of") they are forced to learn. Scolding her children seems to rob her of what little energy she has, and she soon fades from the scene.

Gradgrind and Bounderby are mystified. How could Thomas and Louisa be tempted to go to the circus when they have never been allowed anything that might have spurred their imaginations? Bounderby suggests that it might be Sissy Jupe who's responsible. Louisa met her when Sissy applied for entrance to the school at the Gradgrind home.

The two men decide to see Sissy and her father to try to nip in the bud their influence on Louisa. While Gradgrind searches for their address, Bounderby slips into the children's study. There he finds Louisa, Tom, and their sister Jane and brothers Adam Smith and Malthus.

NOTE: The two youngest Gradgrind boys are named after famous eighteenth-century economists. Adam Smith was the author of an influential book, *The Wealth of Nations* (1776), and Malthus wrote the *Essay on Population* (1798), which argued that war and medical epidemics were necessary to curb the growing world population. Dickens found both writers to be harmful influences.

Bounderby offers his and Gradgrind's forgiveness for the children's "crime" and asks Louisa for a kiss. She passively allows him to kiss her, but when he leaves she vigorously rubs the spot. She tells Tom that she wouldn't cry if he were to take a knife and cut the spot from her face.

Louisa's behavior may make you think of her as a spoiled brat. But from what you have seen of her upbringing, do you understand her attitude? Yet why is she so hostile to Bounderby? The reasons for her coldness toward him will become clearer as the story unfolds.

CHAPTER V

Bounderby and Gradgrind pass through Coketown on their way to find the Jupes. It is a depressing and ugly town, full of harsh noises and foul smells. The red bricks of the building have been blackened by smoke that pours like "interminable serpents" from sooty chimneys. All of the buildings are monotonously similar, and the piston of the huge steam engine moves up and down "like the head of an elephant."

The images of the serpentlike smoke and the steam engine that resembles an elephant's head will be used throughout the novel to indicate the mark that industry has placed on the town, which has become like a jungle.

There are eighteen churches in Coketown that no one attends, despite a committee that argues in Parliament that the citizens should be forced to go to services. Other committees testify that the citizens drink too much, take opium, go to sleazy hangouts to sing and dance. As for Bounderby and Gradgrind, they see the people as lazy and ungrateful, dissatisfied no matter what is done for them. Dickens wonders if there is any relation between these citizens, dulled by their boring, impoverished lives, and the melancholy Gradgrind children. Both the citizens and the children have been denied "fancy." Dickens merely raises the question here, but there is little doubt about the conclusion he implies.

Dickens calls this chapter "The Keynote," which is the note or tone on which a musical composition is based. It is important to Dickens that we understand the conditions that affect the lives of Coketown citizens if we are to understand his book and the anger that caused him to write it.

Bounderby and Gradgrind are surprised to see Sissy Jupe running toward them. Chasing her is the colorless Bitzer, teasing her about her definition of a horse. Gradgrind scolds Bitzer for taunting the girl and then asks her to lead him and Bounderby to the hotel where the performers are staying.

Notice the difference between Bounderby and Gradgrind in this scene and the one that follows. Although they are portrayed as friends, there are distinct differences in personality between them. Which of them seems to have the softer side?

CHAPTER VI

The public house where the performers are staying is called Pegasus's Arms.

NOTE: The image of the horse continues to weave its way through the story, first in the classroom, then in Mr. Jupe's occupation, now in the hotel sign—Pegasus, the mythical flying horse. Such a fabled creature would never meet with Gradgrind or Bounderby's approval, but it is too dark for them to see either the sign or the picture inside. Dickens seems to be having fun by dangling these irritants under their noses without allowing the men to see them.

As Bounderby and Gradgrind wait impatiently for Sissy to find her father, they are joined by members of the troupe: Childers, famous for his Wild Huntsman act, and Kidderminster, who helps Childers's act by dressing as an infant. To emphasize the performers' childlike innocence, Dickens has given them names—Childers and Kidderminster—that suggest their youthful spirits. Notice, too, that Kidderminster plays Cupid, the ancient Roman god of love, usually portrayed as a young boy with a bow and arrow.

Many readers consider *Hard Times* to be an allegory, that is, a story whose characters represent or symbolize a concept or idea, usually as a moral lesson. Bounderby is seen to represent the greedy capitalist who profits from the sweat and labor of others; Gradgrind, the politician who adheres strictly to the utilitarian philosophy. The members of Sleary's troupe stand for the carefree, often frivolous side of life that so many in Coketown are denied. As you read, try to decide what Louisa, Bitzer, Sissy, and Stephen Blackpool (whom you will meet soon) represent in this approach to the novel. Ask yourself if some characters seem more obviously symbolic than others—that is, decide which characters are more like real human beings and which seem more like cardboard cutouts that Dickens uses to prove a point.

Childers tells them that Jupe, who does acrobatic tricks on horseback, has been making many mistakes in his performances recently.

NOTE: Dickens uses many obscure theatrical terms—"missing his tip," "banners," "ponging," etc.—but he is careful to explain them in the context of the speeches.

Bounderby is scornful of all of this jargon, and Gradgrind is offended by what he perceives as lack of respect in the performers' attitudes. But Kidderminster and Childers are unimpressed with their disapproval.

One of Dickens's most effective comic tools is the contrast of a self-important character with one who is irreverent and cocky. In this scene, Dickens allows Bounderby to inflate himself with his own pomposity time and again, only to have one of the performers deflate him with a sly remark.

Childers tells them that Jupe has left town, despondent over what he sees as the loss of his talent and agility. He'd rather disappear than have Sissy see him failing.

Bounderby continues to speak scornfully of Jupe, but Childers stops him cold. Bounderby can think what he wants of Jupe, Childers tells him, but he can't express his opinion here, among Jupe's friends. Childers goes on to say that Sissy will never believe her father deserted her; they were too close.

Hearing of the love between Sissy and her father reminds us of what we have seen of Gradgrind and Louisa. What a difference there is between the two families! It's a difference that will take on greater importance in the future.

Gradgrind is in favor of taking Sissy under his wing as an example to Louisa of what the life she has been so curious about—the life of the performers—comes to in the end. Bounderby thinks Gradgrind is simply asking for trouble. As their argument continues, other members of the troupe begin to gather in the room.

Dickens's fondness for these circus people is even clearer here. He speaks of their "gentleness," their "childishness," and of their generosity and readiness to help each other selflessly.

Some readers have charged that Dickens is too sentimental in portraying the lower classes. They are often made to seem so pure and noble that they lack credibility. Do you agree? If you look for realism, these characters might seem too good to be true. But if you see the novel as an allegory, you might agree that they are not meant to represent full-bodied characters, but the alternative to the strict, bloodless theories and practices championed by Bounderby and Gradgrind.

Mr. Sleary, owner of the circus, enters the room. He's so stricken with asthma that he speaks with a terrible lisp. As he quizzes Gradgrind about what might be done for Sissy, she comes in. Sensing immediately that her father is gone, she sobs uncontrollably.

Gradgrind offers to give Sissy a home and an education as long as she makes up her mind immediately and promises not to speak or write to any of her friends from the troupe. Sleary offers her an alternative. She can stay with the troupe, who will love and care for her always. Sissy is torn but decides to go with Gradgrind after he reminds her to think of what her father would want her to do.

Sissy sadly says good-bye to her friends. Sleary's parting words ask her to think with kindness whenever she sees any horse-riding troupe in the future. People can't always be learning and working, he tells her—they must be "amuthed."

Sleary is clearly speaking for Dickens in this speech. "All work and no play makes Jack a dull boy" is an old saying that expresses the same idea. Right now, Bounderby and Gradgrind think very little about what Sleary says, but watch for Gradgrind to learn the wisdom in the words.

CHAPTER VII

Mrs. Sparsit is Bounderby's housekeeper. Connected to the local aristocracy, she married well, but her husband wasted his money and his life on drink, and died young. Now penniless, she is forced to work for Bounderby, who shows her off to the world as a great trophy, proof of how far he has come in the world. Having as housekeeper a woman so well-bred and highborn is a subject of great pride to him, and he is as vocal about the prestige of her past as he is about the poverty of his own upbringing.

Mrs. Sparsit (together with another character who appears later) represents the aristocracy in the allegorical design of the novel. Dickens held this class in great contempt for what he saw as their snobbery, laziness, and self-importance.

At breakfast, Bounderby thinks about Gradgrind's decision to take control of Sissy's future. For the moment Sissy is staying at the Bounderby house to prevent her from influencing Louisa in any harmful way. His thoughts turn to Louisa's brother Tom, whom Bounderby intends to take into the banking business after the youth's education has finished.

NOTE: Characters in Dickens novels are often highlighted by one or two physical features that become their trademarks. Mrs. Sparsit, for example has a "Coriolanian nose," named after Coriolanus, a Roman general of the fifth century B.C. A Roman nose might indicate nobility and power, but not necessarily beauty in Mrs. Sparsit's case. Other examples of these traits include Gradgrind's deep-set "cave-like" eyes, Bitzer's lack of color, Louisa's emotionless expression. See what others you can find as you read the character descriptions.

It's important to note the relationship between Bounderby and Mrs. Sparsit. Bounderby never tires of contrasting their pasts, and Mrs. Sparsit can only agree. Is Bounderby being cruel to remind her of how far she's fallen? Or is he unaware of her feelings, only concerned with boosting his own ego? Whatever point of view you choose, Bounderby does not come off favorably.

Louisa arrives with her father, who announces his decision to take Sissy into his household to look after the ailing Mrs. Gradgrind after school. He will use Sissy as an example of how one so badly raised can still be educated and "formed" into a respectable person. Bounderby repeats his objection to the plan, but as for Louisa, she has

nothing to say, either in favor of Sissy or against
her.

CHAPTER VIII

Dickens opens this chapter with more information about the citizens of Coketown. He begins
with a story of how Louisa was once overheard by
her father to say, "I wonder," and had been sternly
warned by him never to wonder again. The same
warning might well apply to those who live in
Coketown. The "bodies" of people who regulate
their lives can't agree on how these citizens' lives
can be improved. The one thing these bodies *can*
agree on is that the citizens are never to wonder
what their lives might be like. Yet to Gradgrind's
dismay, even though the town library is stocked
with books of fact, the fiction of Defoe and Goldsmith is always more popular than books on mathematics by Euclid and Cocker.

NOTE: Daniel Defoe (1660–1731) was a writer of
popular fiction whose most famous book is *Robinson Crusoe*. Oliver Goldsmith (1730–1774) was a
novelist and playwright whose work Dickens greatly
admired, particularly the novel of English country
life, *The Vicar of Wakefield*. Euclid was an ancient
Greek mathematician celebrated for his work in
geometry. And Cocker was a seventeenth-century
mathematician whose work was printed in so many
editions that the phrase "according to Cocker" began to mean "according to fact." "According to
Cocker" was one of the titles Dickens considered
for this novel.

Dickens here points out the power of literature and man's need for fictional entrance into other worlds. Which do you feel is more necessary for daily life—fact or imagination? If you had an informal debate in your class, which side would you be on?

As Tom and Louisa sit alone before the fireplace, Tom insists that he hates everyone. More than anything, though, Tom hates his home, which he calls the "jaundiced Jail."

NOTE: Jaundice is a blood disease that causes, among other symptoms, yellow skin, a feeling of apathy, and loss of energy. "Jaundiced" can also mean a distorted or prejudiced point of view. Can both of these meanings apply to the Gradgrind household?

Louisa is sorry she can't do more to help Tom out of his depression, but the things that a sister might do—tell stories, sing songs—are forbidden her.

Tom takes hope in his upcoming job at Bounderby's bank. There he'll have revenge on all the facts that have been stuffed down their throats. At Bounderby's he'll have more freedom. When Louisa warns that Bounderby might prove to be tougher than their father, Tom dismisses her fears. He knows how to handle Bounderby; he'll use the old man's affection for Louisa as a means of getting his way.

This is the first time you've seen Tom and Louisa alone. How do you feel about them? Do you sympathize with their plight? They're not the first young people to think of their home as a prison, but having watched Gradgrind you might feel that their unhappiness is more understandable than that of most young people.

Just as Louisa expresses her bewilderment about the future, Mrs. Gradgrind overhears her utter those forbidden words, "I wonder." Mrs. Gradgrind lectures her children in a pale imitation of her husband, but Louisa defends herself by saying that the dying fire reminded her of how short her life will be.

NOTE: Louisa is identified throughout the novel with fire. When we first meet her in Chapter III, she is described as having "a light with nothing to rest upon, a fire with nothing to burn." Now she identifies her future with the fading embers of the fireplace. These images suggest a passion within her that has been given no reason or encouragement to blaze. Watch for other references to fire in relation to this important character.

Mrs. Gradgrind explodes, reminding them of all the advantages they have been given. She ends her tirade with a typical bit of illogic: if only she had never had a family, the children would know what life was like without her!

Mrs. Gradgrind is a minor character in the novel, but she represents another of those that Gradgrind has virtually destroyed with his insistence on facts. She always mouths her husband's opinions, never

her own. Her addled mind offers some comic relief, but her situation is nonetheless serious.

CHAPTER IX

With Gradgrind on one side at home and
M'Choakumchild on the other at school, Sissy has
been thinking of running away. She stays at the
Gradgrind home, sustained only by the hope that
her father will come for her.

Gradgrind can't understand why Sissy refuses
to see her father as a hopeless villain. And
M'Choakumchild reports that she has no talent for
science, mathematics, or history. When asked what
is the first principle of political economy, Sissy re-
plied, "To do unto others as I would that they
should do unto me."

You might recognize Sissy's answer as the Golden
Rule. She has obviously been raised to respect decency and fair play instead of learning the exacting
standards of political economy. But those values
will not serve her well in M'Choakumchild's class.

Sissy, on one of the rare occasions she talks to
Louisa, expresses a wistful desire to be the Gradgrind daughter Louisa, and "know so much."
Louisa can't understand this wish. Sissy is nice to
everyone, helpful in the house, more than Louisa
could ever be.

Pressed by Louisa, Sissy tells of her loving father,
Jupe. He's a clown who used to cry when he
couldn't make audiences laugh. This had begun to
happen more and more frequently. Some might
think him a bit mentally unbalanced, but they do
not know him as Sissy does.

Sissy begins to cry at these memories, and Louisa

comforts her before asking Sissy to recount what happened when her father left her. Sissy speaks tearfully of her father's intense depression and of being sent that day to pick up a bottle of nine-oils. When she returned from her errand, he was gone. She still hopes that every letter Gradgrind carries is from her father.

Does Louisa seem a bit cruel when she presses Sissy to relive painful memories? Perhaps. But this is the first time we have seen her show concern for someone besides Tom. She is intensely curious to find out what a loving relationship between father and daughter is like. Who can blame her? She has seen no example of it in her own home.

From that conversation on, Louisa waits with as much hope as Sissy does whenever Gradgrind holds a letter, and shows as much disappointment when it turns out not to be from Mr. Jupe. Gradgrind attributes Sissy's false hopes to her poor education.

CHAPTER X

In the deepest, darkest corner of Coketown lives Stephen Blackpool, a weaver in one of the factories. Only forty, Stephen looks much older, a consequence of a life filled with tedious work and deprived of pleasure. Neither particularly intelligent nor learned, Stephen is nonetheless honest and hardworking.

NOTE: Stephen is the first of the poor citizens of Coketown we have met. His dreary surname, Blackpool, suggests that his life is as polluted and darkened by the situation in Coketown as are the skies and streams. Allegorically, Stephen represents the working class that Dickens wished to champion, and his is one of the major stories of the novel.

The work day is over, and an ugly rain falls. Stephen waits outside the factory, searching for someone among the crowds. Suddenly he spots her—Rachael, a gentle, attractive woman of thirty-five. They are old friends, and they speak of their deep affection for each other as they walk. Stephen is upset about certain laws, but Rachael urges him not to worry. Yet both agree that life is "a muddle."

NOTE: The use of dialect In an effort to characterize Blackpool as a member of the lower class, Dickens conveys Stephen's words in a crude dialect that's often difficult to read. Most readers agree that Dickens had a "tin ear" for dialect, that he was not successful in capturing the language of these people. You might also wonder why Stephen's dialect is so thick and Rachael's so slight, since they come from the same place. There's no explanation for this contradiction, nor is there an easy way to understand Stephen's lines. You just have to have patience and know that you'll probably get used to the dialect as you read.

Stephen walks Rachael to her home and continues to his little room above a shop.

NOTE: The reference to the undertaker's ladder that appears in Rachael's street is a grim foreshadowing of events to come. It's a characteristic device of Dickens.

When Stephen enters his room, he is surprised and shocked by a woman there. She's dirty, drunk, ugly, dressed in rags. He knows her, and her return causes him great pain. But she merely screeches at him that she'll keep returning again and again. Then she claims his bed as her own and falls into a deep stupor. Stephen is forced to sleep in a chair.

It may seem that the story of Stephen, Rachael, and the mysterious woman has nothing to do with Bounderby and the Gradgrinds. But Dickens is a master at weaving two seemingly separate stories and having them intertwine as the novel unfolds.

This story also brings suspense to the plot, the kind that kept Dickens's weekly readers intrigued. What is Stephen and Rachael's relationship? Who is the witchlike woman? Dickens begins to whet our appetites for the next chapter.

CHAPTER XI

The next morning Stephen is at work in the factory. The government has taken great pains, Dickens tells us, to gauge the capacity of work the machines are capable of producing, but it has ignored the human beings and their suffering.

Some readers feel that Dickens's frequent interruptions are intrusive and delay the action of the story. Do you find these passages preachy or persuasive? Remember that his audience would be reading about issues that were controversial and that affected their daily lives. Dickens's passion for these issues is understandable if you've ever felt strongly about a contemporary issue.

At lunchtime, Stephen goes to Bounderby's house. Bounderby owns the mill where Stephen works. Bounderby is eating lunch and is surprised to see Stephen; there has never been any trouble with this worker (or "hand") before.

Stephen tells the story of the hideous woman. She's his wife, whom he married nineteen years ago. But she began drinking and sold the furniture and clothes to pay for her habit. Despite Stephen's attempts to cure her, her condition worsened. She would wander off, lead a loose, whorish life, and return. Five years ago he paid her to stay away permanently, and he began to resume a normal life—until last night.

Bounderby has heard of Stephen's bad marriage. Mrs. Sparsit asks if the trouble was caused by a difference in Stephen's and his wife's ages.

Why do you think Mrs. Sparsit asks this question so pointedly? And why does Bounderby seem sheepish when she does? This small detail hints at a future plot development.

Stephen wants to divorce his wife, and Bounderby and Mrs. Sparsit are shocked. It can't be done, Bounderby tells him. But Stephen has read of wealthy people ending unsuitable marriages. Why can't he?

NOTE: Divorce in the mid-nineteenth century was almost always the privilege of the rich. Many lawmakers felt that the lower classes didn't need easy divorce, that there was no great demand for it. Dickens had a personal resentment against the divorce laws. Because of their complexity, he was unable to end his own marriage to his wife Catherine in order to marry Ellen Ternan, a woman with whom he was deeply in love. Some of his personal frustration found a voice in Stephen's dilemma (although lack of money was not Dickens's problem).

Stephen is frustrated by Bounderby's stubborn attitude. If Stephen were to hurt his wife or desert her or marry another, a law would *punish* him. Why is there no law to *help* him out of this terrible situation?

Stephen's contempt for the law angers Bounderby, who tells him that the law is not Stephen's concern. Millwork is his concern. Marrying that woman was just a bad piece of luck that he'll have to live with.

This scene dramatizes the relationship between management and labor. Coming to ask for help, Stephen only gets accused of being a troublemaker. He should stay in his place, he's told, and make the best of his bad luck.

CHAPTER XII

Saddened and discouraged, Stephen heads home. On the way, he's met by an elderly woman, just arrived in town after a long trip. She's seen him leaving Bounderby's house and she asks about that man. How does he look? Is he healthy? The woman is grateful for Stephen's answers. As she walks with him, she tells him she makes the 40-mile trip from her home to Coketown every year just to catch a glimpse of Bounderby.

Stephen is curious about the old woman's interest in Bounderby, but he doesn't inquire. Instead, she asks questions about his life in the factory, assuming that all is well with the workers there. Stephen doesn't shatter her illusions. Later, at his work, Stephen glances out the window to see her staring with admiration at the factory buildings.

NOTE: In addition to the images of the serpent (the smoke) and the elephant (the steam engine), Dickens often refers to the factories as the Fairy Palaces because, from a distance, they look magical when lighted. Obviously the image is heavy with irony, since few places are less magical than the factories.

After work, Stephen wanders sorrowfully in the rain, dreading to go home and face his wife. How, he wonders, can someone as good and kind as Rachael have a fate determined by such a terrible woman as his wife? His thoughts become more fatalistic as he nears home.

CHAPTER XIII

Thinking of the inequality with which Death chooses its victims, Stephen enters his room to find Rachael at his wife's bedside, treating the drunken woman's sores with medication from a bottle. Rachael has known Stephen's wife since they were young girls and was a friend to the couple when they were first married. She is helping the unfortunate creature because she can't stand to see anyone suffer.

Stephen's wife is close to unconsciousness, and according to the doctor, will be in this state until tomorrow. When Stephen spots the bottle of medicine, he trembles with fright to see that its contents are poisonous if swallowed.

It's easy to realize that Stephen is having morbid thoughts of killing his wife. When the opportunity is in front of him, in the guise of the bottle of poison, he is shaken with fear at what he has been thinking.

Stephen falls into a gradual sleep, interrupted by a disturbing dream. A wedding ceremony, in which he is the groom and an unknown woman is the bride, is interrupted by a great shaft of light that illuminates a line from the ten commandments to the altar. Suddenly the wedding turns into a funeral service and burial, with Stephen as the corpse and witnessed by a group that seems to represent the entire world.

Why does Stephen have this terrible dream? Which commandment—the one forbidding adultery or the one forbidding murder—is illuminated on the tablet? Whatever your opinion on which issue Stephen feels more guilty about, it's clear that he feels condemned by God for his thoughts.

When he awakens, he sees that Rachael is asleep. His wife stirs on the bed as he watches from the chair. She grasps for the bottle, perhaps thinking it's liquor, and begins to open it. He has no will to try to stop her, subconsciously hoping that she will drink the poison, but Rachael awakens in time and wrenches the bottle from her grasp.

Some readers fault Dickens for excessive emotionalism in scenes such as this; they find the scenes overly sentimental and melodramatic. Whether you feel that this scene is moving or overdone is probably a matter of personal taste. Remember that the readers of Dickens's day loved such sensational elements as long-lost wives, bottles of poison, warning dreams, tearful declarations of love. (And tastes haven't changed much, if we can judge from the popularity of today's soap operas!) As a popular novelist, Dickens gave the public what it wanted.

CHAPTER XIV

Time has passed, and Gradgrind, now a member of Parliament, decides that young Tom should work at Bounderby's bank. He discontinues Sissy's education, feeling that she has no head for learning. Sissy sadly agrees. She is kept on, however, as an indispensable member of the household.

Gradgrind has plans for Louisa as well, and Tom tells her that these plans have something to do with Bounderby. Tom reminds her of their own close relationship (even though he sees little of her now that he's working), and Louisa agrees to remember how much they mean to each other.

NOTE: Dickens's use of metaphors   At the end of this chapter, Dickens compares Time to a weaver, spinning threads that become a woman. What kind of woof would he weave now? Louisa wonders. ("Woof" is a weaving term meaning texture or fabric.) Dickens writes, "But, his factory is a secret place, his work is noiseless, and his Hands are mutes." This kind of comparison is known as an "extended metaphor." Two different things are being compared (Time and a weaver) as in a regular metaphor. But the metaphor is extended to include other parallels: the woof becomes the pattern of Louisa's future, the place Time works is a silent factory, his workers are mute hands, etc. The extended metaphor is one of Dickens's most famous stylistic traits.

CHAPTER XV

Gradgrind tells Louisa that Bounderby has proposed marriage. This news can't be too surprising to you, given the number of hints about it up to now. Even Mrs. Sparsit has anticipated it, as evidenced by her comments to Bounderby about the troubles known to come to marriages of "unequal ages."

Louisa allows no emotion but merely asks her father a series of questions: Does he think she loves Bounderby? Does he ask her to love Bounderby? Does Bounderby ask her to love him? Gradgrind is uncomfortable, suggesting that the matter of love may be out of place. Love is "fancy"; it is sentimental. Bounderby is too aware of Louisa's upbringing to raise such an issue.

This is the first time you've seen Gradgrind uncomfortable. Louisa's questions about love find him completely off guard. Why does he react this way?

Did he expect that Louisa would be overcome with joy at the prospect of marrying Bounderby? Or is it possible that he himself is uneasy about arranging this marriage? Your answer might depend on whether you feel that Gradgrind has a human side.

Louisa responds strangely. She talks of the fires of the Coketown chimney, saying that the "languid and monotonous" smoke by day gives way to fire at night. Then she says that she is "satisfied" to accept Bounderby's offer.

NOTE: Louisa's allusion to the Coketown chimney is another example of her connection to fire. It suggests that she is aware of the youthful passion that lies within her and will never be allowed to express itself. Why is the reference lost on her father? It is a plea from the heart to save her from future unhappiness, but Gradgrind is either blind or insensitive. Some readers have found this scene hard to believe. No father, they say, could be that unaware of his daughter's feelings. But the marriage is a necessary plot device, and Gradgrind's stony reaction—believable or not—is important to making it happen.

Gradgrind wonders if Louisa has accepted any other secret proposal, but Louisa says she hasn't. How could she, with her education, have secret dreams or hopes? Her answer pleases Gradgrind, and they go to break the news to Louisa's mother, who wishes her joy. But Sissy is shocked and saddened. When she looks at Louisa to try to see what is going on in her mind, Louisa becomes cold and aloof and pulls away from the girl.

CHAPTER XVI

Bounderby is nervous about breaking the news of the upcoming wedding to Mrs. Sparsit. He fully expects hysteria from her when she learns she will be replaced in the household. But Mrs. Sparsit reacts with a mixture of condescension and sympathy. She turns down his offer to stay as part of the household, but accepts an apartment in his bank and a similar stipend to what she has been receiving.

Bounderby is frustrated at her calm. Her tone suggests that she predicts only misery for the couple, and he feels very much the victim.

The wedding takes place after a period of loveless "courtship." Bounderby's speech at the wedding breakfast is a masterpiece of self-praise and practicality.

As Louisa is ready to leave on her honeymoon, Tom takes her aside to praise her for being such a good sport about marrying Bounderby. For the first time, Louisa begins to show emotion underneath her facade, but Tom doesn't notice. He's just pleased with the thought of how much more pleasant life will be in the future.

NOTE: This chapter marks the end of the first book, entitled "Sowing." To sow is to plant seeds, and Dickens uses farming terms in the titles of all three books. "Sowing" suggests the seeds planted by Gradgrind in the raising of his children. Both

Tom and Louisa have been raised according to strict principles. But what will become of the harvest when the seeds are fully grown? Will Gradgrind be pleased with his "crop"? Or will the harvest be a bitter one? And what will become of Stephen Blackpool? The title of the second book, "Reaping," tells us that we will soon know.

BOOK THE SECOND

CHAPTER I

It's a sunny day in Coketown, which, seen from afar, seems only a "blur of soot and smoke."

NOTE: Dickens is something of a prophet for his belief that industrial smoke and waste were unhealthy to the environment and to people. It was not until well into the twentieth century that the full effects of pollution were recognized and laws passed to prevent industrial abuse of the air and water.

On this stifling day, Mrs. Sparsit sits at the window of her apartment at the bank. She now has a deaf maid to attend to her and the assistance of the bank's light porter (messenger), who is none other than Sissy's old headache, Bitzer. Mrs. Sparsit is indulging in one of her favorite pastimes—pitying Bounderby for his marriage, now a year old.

When Bitzer brings her tea, the two gossip. Bitzer

has little to report, only that the mill workers are planning a trade union, which Mrs. Sparsit finds disgraceful. She suggests firing anyone who attempts to join such a union, but Bitzer says that tactic has failed.

Mrs. Sparsit represents those of the upper classes who felt threatened by workers joining together to act as one. It is a prejudice that some employers still hold, no doubt.

Bitzer acts as a spy for Mrs. Sparsit. We learn that his own mother is in a workhouse, allowed only half a pound of tea a year from her generous son.

Bitzer's other bit of gossip concerns young Tom Gradgrind, whom he hates. Bitzer finds him lazy, untrustworthy, useless. He also has unkind words for the millworkers, whom he considers spendthrifts and pleasure seekers.

Don't forget that Bitzer is one of Gradgrind's prize pupils, who represents for Dickens another result of such an education. Bitzer is smug, sneaky, selfish.

A young, handsome man has arrived to see Mrs. Sparsit. He has with him a letter of introduction to Bounderby from Gradgrind, whom he met in London. The well-bred stranger knows just how to flatter Mrs. Sparsit, and she is soon putty in his hands. After making inquiries about Mrs. Bounderby's age, he asks directions to the Bounderby house.

After he leaves, Mrs. Sparsit comments favorably on the gentleman. Bitzer suggests that he looks like he "games" (gambles), and both voice their disapproval of the habit. When Bitzer leaves, she sits alone at the window until Bitzer announces dinner. At her solitary meal, the only words that escape her lips are, "O, you fool."

Mrs. Sparsit's "fool" is undoubtedly addressed to Bounderby, since she spends most of her time thinking about him. Why does she care so much? Her behavior is not easy to explain, as you shall see.

The gentleman is yet another stranger added to the story. Why is he in London? Why does he inquire about Mrs. Bounderby? Dickens continues to build his suspenseful plot.

CHAPTER II

The political party to which Gradgrind belongs needs recruits. One of these recruits happens to be the younger brother of a fine gentleman. The younger man has tried a variety of occupations and diversions—cavalry officer, assistant to an ambassador, yachtsman—and found them all boring. Meeting Gradgrind and his political cronies (the "Hard Fact fellows"), the young man impressed them. They decided to send him to Coketown to meet influential people there. And that is how James Harthouse found himself at Bounderby's that sunny day.

Harthouse meets with Bounderby, who immediately sets him straight about Coketown. The smoke, says Bounderby, is good for the lungs, and mill work is the most pleasant and easy work there is. As for the workers, all they want is to eat venison and turtle soup with a gold spoon! No matter what Harthouse might have heard, these are the facts—according to Bounderby.

When Harthouse meets Louisa, he is immediately attracted to her, particularly to the emotions that lie buried beneath her cool exterior.

Harthouse is a man without a fixed opinion or philosophy. He supports the Gradgrind party because it is the first one that accepted him. One set of ideas is as good as the next to him.

The more time Harthouse spends with Bounderby, the more bored he becomes. But one thing keeps him from abandoning this newfound political life: the intriguing thought of bringing some expression to Louisa's beautiful, passive face. Harthouse observes at dinner that Tom is the only person she cares for. Thinking that Tom is his key to unlocking Louisa's heart, Harthouse allows the young man to show him to his hotel.

CHAPTER III

Dickens makes no secret of his contempt for Tom—he's a hypocrite, a monster. Harthouse holds him in contempt as well but has his own uses for Tom. He invites him to his room for a rare treat, a drink and a smoke.

NOTE: Harthouse's private term for Tom is "the whelp," a slang term for a young person, derived from the word used to describe the offspring of a dog, lion, bear, or other carnivorous mammal.

Harthouse eggs Tom on about his sister and Bounderby. Tom, smoking, drinking, and feeling important, is an easy target. He tells Harthouse that Louisa doesn't care for Bounderby and never did. Tom had persuaded her to marry the man to make his own life easier. But he doesn't worry about Louisa. She has powerful hidden resources, although he admits she's as innocent and unsophisticated as when she first left home.

Tom drifts off to sleep from the powerful effects of the alcohol and tobacco. When he awakens and Harthouse sends him home, Tom feels he has been influenced by this new friend in an unusual way. If only he knew what the influence would mean, Dickens tells us, he might have jumped in the river and ended his life once and for all.

Dickens's final comment lets us know that Harthouse is up to no good. The mystery of Harthouse and what he will mean to Louisa and Bounderby continues.

CHAPTER IV

In a public hall in Coketown, a man named Slackbridge gives a passionate speech to a group of mill workers. He tells them that the time has come for them to join together and throw off the oppression that has suffocated them for so long— the oppression of the mill owners. Only when the workers are united in brotherhood, says Slackbridge, will they share the "glorious rights of Humanity."

There is a visible contrast between the speaker and the audience. He is "ill-made," with a continual sour expression; they are honest, sensible, good-humored. They hang on his every word because they sincerely feel that their lives can be made better and that Slackbridge might have the solution.

Slackbridge singles out one man for ridicule. This

is a man who refuses to join the union, despite its benefits to the workers. Many boo at the reference to this man, but others insist that he be allowed to speak. The chairman of the meeting interrupts Slackbridge's tirade and introduces the outcast— Stephen Blackpool.

Stephen tells the audience that he's convinced the union will do more harm than good. But he also has a personal reason for not joining, one he can't share with them. The chairman urges him to think again before making a final decision, but Stephen has made up his mind. He knows that the rules demand he be shunned by the rest of the workers. He's willing to accept their avoidance of him, but he hopes he'll be allowed to keep his job. With that, he leaves the hall. Slackbridge takes to the podium again, to fire up the audience. The workers are soon cheering. Only a few feel guilty about their treatment of Stephen.

The next few days are solitary and painful for Stephen. The workers follow their pledge and won't speak to him or acknowledge his presence on the street. He begins to avoid Rachael, afraid that she would be shunned by the factory women.

NOTE: Although women worked in the factory, they had no say in the forming of the union. Only men were allowed to vote in these matters or in any election.

A few days after the union meeting, Stephen is stopped on the street by Bitzer, who tells him that Bounderby wants to see him right away.

NOTE: Dickens's view of unions   The union meeting pictured in this chapter is crude and melodramatic. You might wonder from this portrayal if Dickens hated unions as much as he hated the mill owners. Some readers feel that the scene was added in response to those who felt that management was treated too harshly in the earlier chapters. Since *Hard Times* was a serial, Dickens could easily have added a scene to placate those critics. Others feel that Dickens was trying to show that there is evil on both sides. While management was filled with greedy taskmasters, unions were often run by demagogues (men who seize power by arousing people's emotions and prejudices). Dickens's sympathies were clearly for the working man and woman, unavoidably caught between two strong forces. In short, Dickens believed in the worth of the human being, not the worth of institutions easily corrupted.

CHAPTER V

Arriving at Bounderby's house, Stephen is ushered into the drawing room, where Bounderby, Louisa, and Harthouse are gathered. Bounderby demands to hear about the Combination (union), and he is outraged at Stephen's silence.

Bounderby wants Stephen to denounce Slackbridge as a troublemaker. Stephen is sorry that Slackbridge has power over the workers, but poor leadership is all these people are ever offered.

Stephen then offers a moving defense of the mill workers as honest, hardworking, and faithful.

Bounderby is merely frustrated, not moved. He urges Stephen to list for Harthouse the workers' complaints, and he does: poor conditions, long hours, management that treats them as numbers, not people. Getting rid of Slackbridge—or one hundred Slackbridges—won't help. Things will still be "a muddle."

Bounderby concludes that Stephen is one of those workers who always have a complaint, and fires him. Stephen reminds Bounderby that if he can't get work in Coketown, no one else will hire him either. His pleas seem to affect only Louisa, but she says nothing. Stephen leaves the house, praying for heaven to help the world.

NOTE: This scene between Bounderby and Stephen may seem forced and long-winded to you. If so, you're not alone. Rather than a conversation between two people, it seems more a debate between figures representing management and labor. Readers have pointed out that Stephen does not speak like a mill worker and is too obviously Dickens's mouthpiece. Dickens the reformer seems to have overwhelmed Dickens the novelist.

CHAPTER VI

Leaving Bounderby's, Stephen is surprised to see Rachael walking with the mysterious woman he had met a year before. The old woman wanted to catch a glimpse of Mrs. Bounderby, and Stephen reports that Louisa is young and beautiful, but silently he doubts that the two are as happily married as the woman assures him they are.

Stephen tells Rachael of his dismissal from the factory. His only comfort is that his departure from Coketown will make life easier for Rachael. No one will now treat her badly for being his friend.

Stephen asks the old woman to his house for tea. The woman tells Rachael and Stephen her name—Mrs. Pegler. She is a widow whose husband has been long dead. She once had a son who did very well for himself, but he is "lost" to her.

There's a knock at the door. Hearing the name "Bounderby," Mrs. Pegler panics and insists on hiding.

Louisa enters with Tom. Until now she has thought of the mill workers as a group of faceless employees, never as individuals. This is the first time she has seen how simply they live.

She has come to offer whatever help she can. She can't believe Stephen is to be "sacrificed" because of the prejudices of labor and management. Louisa then guesses correctly that the promise keeping Stephen out of the union was made to Rachael.

NOTE: The exact nature of this promise is never made clear, and some readers point to its flimsiness as a plot device that creates a major weakness in the Stephen Blackpool plot.

Louisa offers money to Stephen, but he'll accept only one pound (several dollars). He's grateful for her kindness, but too proud to accept more.

What a change we see in Louisa! Her behavior is often perplexing, alternately sweet and cold. Now, for the first time, she extends herself selflessly to someone else. Through Stephen she is learning that people are more than the statistics her father always made them out to be.

Tom pulls Stephen aside and offers him a chance to do a favor for him and benefit from it. All Stephen has to do is hang around the bank for an hour or two after work. Bitzer will meet him with a message. Assured by Stephen that such a favor will be to his advantage, Stephen agrees.

What does Tom have up his sleeve? Is it likely he wants to help Stephen? Has Tom had a change of heart like Louisa? If so, why does he make a point to speak to Stephen privately?

For the next two days, Stephen fulfills his promise and waits outside the bank after his work at the factory is finished. He sees Bitzer, but the colorless porter says nothing. Stephen decides to wait two hours on the third day. Observed only by Mrs. Sparsit, he lingers patiently until darkness falls. When no message comes, he returns home, sleeps a bit, then prepares to leave town before the other workers are awake.

Making a detour only to pass Rachael's house, Stephen heads out of town, looking back to see Coketown awaken. With a heavy heart, thinking of Rachael, he walks into the countryside and an uncertain future.

NOTE: Stephen Blackpool It has been noted that Stephen is named after St. Stephen, a Christian martyr, because he too is a martyr—to the cause of the oppressed worker. Readers have faulted Dickens for hopelessly stacking the deck against Stephen: a drunken, whorish wife; a woman he loves but can't marry; fellow workers who avoid him; the loss of his job; and the need to leave home. Does he have any chance faced with these odds? In his attempt to show the abused worker, Dickens might have created a character so pitiful that he's no longer believable. In a pure allegory, the portrayal of Stephen might work more successfully. But in a novel that tries for realism, he strikes many as one of its weaker links. What do you think? What might Dickens have done to make Stephen a more realistic character?

CHAPTER VII

With a bit of political coaching and a natural talent for hypocrisy, Harthouse does very well as a representative of the Gradgrind party. When he openly declares his cynical philosophy to Louisa, she is not shocked; she was raised with attitudes like these. The more she sees of humanity, the more she feels that nothing matters. Although she struggles to find a more hopeful side to life, Harthouse's cynicism overwhelms her.

Harthouse is spending a great deal of time at the Bounderby home, still diverted by the challenge of making Louisa care for him. He watches and observes everything about her, hoping for a clue to win her affections.

The Bounderbys now live in a large house in the country outside of town. Bounderby obtained the house as a result of a bank foreclosure, and he takes great delight in making fun of its expensive furnishings and art objects. He reminds everyone that he has no use for such finery, since he was once poor and unaccustomed to the trappings of wealth.

Have you ever known anyone who sneered at something and at the same time couldn't resist it? Bounderby is that kind of snob and hypocrite. He is attracted to what money can buy but is vocal in his disapproval of it.

On a summer afternoon, Harthouse runs into Louisa in one of her favorite private places, a clearing in the woods. During the conversation, he correctly guesses that Tom has been gambling and that Louisa has been paying his debts. She admits that Tom did borrow a great deal of money from her after she was first married. Since then she's given him occasional small sums, and recently he's asked for an amount she can't afford. His behavior worries her.

Harthouse offers to use his influence to help Tom if it will help Louisa feel less anxious about him.

We know that Harthouse is lying. He has no interest in Tom's well-being. He may even be encouraging Tom to spend beyond his means.

Tom is depressed over his finances. Alone with Harthouse, he confesses his debts. He's upset that Louisa's marriage hasn't been as profitable for him as he had hoped. Harthouse offers free advice whenever Tom should need it. In exchange, he asks that Tom be kinder to Louisa in the future.

That night, Tom apologizes to his sister for his recent sullen behavior. Louisa is grateful to Harthouse for his help, and now Harthouse observes that she finally has a smile for someone other than Tom.

By using Louisa's love for Tom, Harthouse comes closer to seducing her, not out of love for her, but out of boredom. Tom has gambled himself deeply into debt, and the results of his carelessness remain to be seen. The gunpowder of this chapter's title is about to be ignited.

CHAPTER VIII

The next morning Harthouse sits at his window and ponders the success he's had in drawing Louisa to him. She is now in his confidence, and he in hers. Louisa's indifference to her husband and her feeling that Harthouse knows the deepest secrets of her soul have made him important to her. Harthouse doesn't know the results of his manipulations. What will be, will be, he tells himself.

NOTE: Dickens seems to feel that Harthouse is the greater villain for having no specific aim for his wickedness: "It is the drifting icebergs . . . that wreck the ships." His actions spring from boredom, not from the impulse to destroy. But destroy he does.

At Bounderby's later that day, Harthouse learns that the bank has been robbed of 150 pounds. Bounderby reports that Louisa fainted when she heard the news; he thinks it speaks well of her to be so concerned for his money.

You know that Louisa could care less about the money. Why does she react so strongly? Is it possible she suspects Tom? She knows he needs money and is often unprincipled. Her love for him makes her suspicions unbearable.

Bounderby thinks the chief suspect is Stephen Blackpool. Not only has Stephen characterized himself as a dissatisfied worker, but he was seen by Mrs. Sparsit to linger around the bank three nights in a row. He's also been seen talking to a strange old woman who seems to have disappeared.

It's certain now that Tom is responsible for the theft. It was he who asked Stephen to wait outside the bank on those evenings. The suspicion that falls on Mrs. Pegler is also worth noting. Her function in the book is still a mystery (although you may have guessed her identity), and Dickens is preparing us for a surprise.

Mrs. Sparsit is invited to stay with the Bounderbys in order to soothe her frazzled nerves. There she offers hints that the Bounderby marriage is a mistake. She takes care of Bounderby as she used to, plays backgammon with him, makes him his favorite drink—things Louisa doesn't do.

The suggestion is there that Mrs. Sparsit wants to marry Bounderby, but we never know this for certain. Maybe she wants life the way it used to be when she was his housekeeper. Which do you think is more likely?

That night Louisa pleads with Tom to tell her if he has anything to confess. Tom has nothing to say. When she reminds him of the private words he had with Stephen when they visited the latter's room, Tom lies and says he was only warning him to make good use of Louisa's money. Louisa leaves, and Tom throws himself on his pillow. He cries for lying to his sister, but he's not sorry, and he condemns all that's good in the world.

Tom's emotional reaction shows that he's aware of how badly he's treated Louisa. Yet he's not sorry for what he's done; he's had no change of heart, and he feels no remorse for casting suspicion on the innocent Stephen.

CHAPTER IX

As Mrs. Sparsit recuperates at the Bounderbys, she continues to prowl about the house, making sure that she goes unnoticed. She is particularly interested in the goings-on between Harthouse and Louisa, suspecting that their relationship is warming.

Bitzer arrives with news that Louisa's mother is dying and requests to see her. Louisa makes immediate preparations to go home, where she has gone rarely since her marriage. There is little for her there. Mrs. Gradgrind has been constantly ill, Louisa's sisters are not close to her, and she is still estranged from Sissy.

Louisa finds her mother cared for by Sissy (now an "equal" in the household) and Louisa's younger sister Jane. Louisa notices with some discomfort that Jane is closer to Sissy than to Louisa. Jane seems happier than she ever was, and Louisa wonders how much of that happiness is due to Sissy's influence.

Mrs. Gradgrind is barely conscious, but she rallies when she realizes that Louisa is there. The dying woman has a few last words for her daughter. Mrs. Gradgrind knows that something has been missing in her children's education. They have learned many "ologies," but one seems to have been forgotten. As the old woman gropes in vain for the missing "ology," she dies.

What is the "ology" Mrs. Gradgrind was trying to remember? Or was she simply rattling on in her dying state? Dickens offers no specific clue, but if you were asked what was missing from the Gradgrind children's education, what would you say? Love? Imagination? Sympathy? The answer is left for you to decide.

CHAPTER X

Weeks pass, and Mrs. Sparsit is still at the Bounderby house. She continues her two-faced attitude to Bounderby, praising him to his face but calling him a "noodle" behind his back. Resolved not to lose sight of the flattering Mrs. Sparsit—and partly to irritate Louisa—Bounderby invites her back for future weekend visits.

Mrs. Sparsit, ever observant, begins to see Louisa's progress into adultery in concrete terms—as a descent down a staircase that has a "dark pit of shame and ruin at the bottom."

The robbery is still very much on everyone's mind, but there has been no luck in finding Stephen or the old woman implicated in the crime.

As Mrs. Sparsit is packing to return home, she looks out her window to see Louisa and Harthouse talking in the garden. Mrs. Sparsit sees Louisa's hair almost touch his face as they lean in to talk quietly—close enough for Mrs. Sparsit to feel that Louisa is moving further down the "staircase."

She can't hear their conversation, but if she could, she would hear them discussing the robbery. Harthouse assures Louisa that Stephen is guilty, that Harthouse recognized the man as a hypocrite from the very first. The robbery was obviously committed out of anger for Bounderby's treatment of Stephen, Harthouse tells her.

Mrs. Sparsit gathers whatever news she can of Harthouse and Louisa, even after she moves back to her own home. She waits eagerly for the final descent, certain that it's just a matter of time.

CHAPTER XI

As Louisa continues down the "staircase," Gradgrind arrives from London to bury his wife in a "businesslike manner." Mrs. Sparsit maintains her relentless scrutiny, even to the point of looking through personal letters for a clue. But nothing happens.

Bounderby goes away on business but insists that Mrs. Sparsit spend her usual weekend at his house, no matter what objections Louisa might have.

Before Mrs. Sparsit leaves for the country, she pumps Tom for information regarding Harthouse. Tom tells her that Harthouse is away on a hunting trip, but that he expects Harthouse to be at the Bounderbys on Sunday. Mrs. Sparsit then asks Tom to tell Louisa that she won't be coming to the Bounderbys for the weekend after all.

Mrs. Sparsit is laying a trap for Louisa. She thinks that Louisa and Harthouse are planning a rendezvous while Bounderby is out of town. Mrs. Sparsit cancels her own trip in order to give the couple the chance to be alone—and therefore enough rope to hang themselves.

The next day, from a discreet hiding place, Mrs. Sparsit watches Tom at the train station, where he is supposed to meet Harthouse. When Harthouse doesn't arrive, Mrs. Sparsit knows why. Harthouse asked Tom to meet him there as a diversion so that he could slip off alone to the country house.

As it begins to rain, Mrs. Sparsit hurries across town to the country house, all the while imagining Louisa "very near the bottom" of the staircase.

Creeping through the shrubbery to the house, Mrs. Sparsit peers through the window, but all is quiet. She moves to the nearby woods and there finds what she's looking for: Harthouse, with his arms around Louisa! He tells her of his love for her, but Louisa turns away from him time and again. Plans are made between them, but the steadily increasing rain keeps Mrs. Sparsit from hearing them. She is certain, however, that they arrange to meet later that night.

Paying little attention to the fact that Louisa appeared to discourage Harthouse's advances, Mrs. Sparsit is certain that Louisa has finally fallen into the abyss. Cold and drenched to the skin, Mrs. Sparsit is nonetheless triumphant. That sneaking through bushes and standing in the rain to eavesdrop might be beneath her dignity—and her proud pedigree—never occurs to her. She is obsessed with finding Louisa guilty.

Still crouching in the shrubbery, Mrs. Sparsit sees Louisa leave the house. Certain that the young woman is about to elope, Mrs. Sparsit follows her to the railroad station and gets on the same train. Mrs. Sparsit assumes that Louisa is on her way to Coketown. She rides to that stop, only to get off the train and find Louisa is nowhere to be seen. Louisa has left the train at an earlier stop and Mrs. Sparsit has lost her!

NOTE: Notice how Dickens adds to the tension and suspense of these scenes by setting them in the midst of a rainstorm. Many readers see a parallel between the storm outside and the inner lives of the characters. As the storm rises, so do Mrs. Sparsit's expectations that she will finally see Louisa disgraced. And the mounting violence of the storm also suggests the rising passion between Harthouse and Louisa. The events of the chapter would mean the same without the storm, but they are more vivid and exciting because of Dickens's masterly touch. Watch how the storm continues to add tension in the next chapter.

CHAPTER XII

Gradgrind, home for vacation, watches the storm wondering if the lightning outside will strike one of the Coketown chimneys.

NOTE: You are reminded by Gradgrind's musing of Louisa's identification with fire throughout the novel. It was in Book the First, Chapter 15, that she looked to the chimneys and noted the fire within them. Gradgrind's concern that the chimneys might be struck by lightning immediately foreshadows Louisa's entrance with news that will appall him.

As the thunder booms and the rain pours, Louisa enters, drenched and breathless. She wastes no time in telling him why she is there. She denounces her upbringing, accusing her father of taking from her everything that made life more than a "conscious death."

She asks him if he remembers the last time they spoke in this room (when he told her of Bounderby's proposal). If he had given her one bit of encouragement at the time, she would have told him what she is telling him now, of her fears and dreams and hopes. Could he then have allowed her to marry such a man as Bounderby? Gradgrind, shaken, answers that he could not.

She tells him that Harthouse is the first person to understand her. She isn't sure if she loves him, but he loves her and waits for her now. She begs her father for his help now, since all his past teaching and philosophy have proved useless to her. What can he offer her now? As she pleads with him, she falls to the ground in a faint.

Book the Second thus ends with Louisa, a prime product of the Gradgrind/Bounderby school of thought, miserable and wretchedly unhappy. This is the "reaping," or harvest, of the seeds sown in the first book. Gradgrind has come face to face with the failure of his daughter's upbringing (and has yet to discover that his son is a thief). Bounderby has been deserted by his wife. Think back to the ending of the first book. Both men were smug about this marriage, but now they must reap what they have sown and are both the worse for it. As for Stephen, he has been forced to leave his home, and by doing so is falsely accused of a crime.

BOOK THE THIRD

NOTE: "Garnering" is the name of Book the Third. To "garner" is to "store up" the results of a harvest. We have seen the reaping of the Bounderby and Gradgrind "crops," and the harvesting that resulted in Louisa's failed marriage and Tom's crime. Now, in this final book, you will see what is "garnered"—taken home to store for the future—by the main characters.

CHAPTER I

Louisa wakes up in her old room, weak and in pain. She learns from Jane that Sissy brought her here and stayed the night at her bedside.

Gradgrind comes into Louisa's room, saddened and inarticulate. He can scarcely express his regret to Louisa for what has happened to her. This is a remarkable admission for a man as proud as Gradgrind. We have seen brief glimpses of a human being in his behavior before, but he is now truly a changed man. Dickens attests to his sincerity in this scene, saying that Gradgrind "meant to do great things." Elsewhere, Dickens wrote: ". . . there is reason and good intention in much that he does—but . . . he overdoes it."

Do you expect a similar change of heart from Bounderby?

Louisa is moved by her father's response, saying that she doesn't blame him and never will. But Gradgrind has no advice in regard to Harthouse.

Gradgrind has heard that there is a wisdom of the head and a wisdom of the heart, but he is not sure if that is true. He had always thought the head was sufficient to solve all problems.

Gradgrind's reference to the heart and the head points to one of the novel's major themes—the need to balance intelligence and emotion to achieve happiness.

Sissy comes in as Gradgrind leaves. Louisa pretends to be asleep; she's upset that Sissy should see her so distraught. Then she feels Sissy's tears on her face and is moved that anyone should care for her so deeply. When Sissy offers her love, the dams of emotion burst inside Louisa. She asks Sissy's forgiveness as the two embrace warmly.

Sissy represents the wisdom of the heart that Gradgrind is not sure exists. Louisa has been leaning in the heart's direction for a long time, but her upbringing and pride have kept her at a distance. As she embraces Sissy, she symbolically embraces the power of love and all that it can accomplish.

CHAPTER II

Harthouse waits impatiently for Louisa, mystified that she hasn't appeared or sent word to him. Frustrated, he searches for her in vain. Harthouse returns to the hotel to continue his anxious waiting.

Word of Louisa soon comes, delivered by Sissy. She faces Harthouse without fear or agitation and tells him that Louisa will never see him again as long as she lives. Harthouse is dumbstruck, not only by the news but by the purity of the soul that delivers it.

Harthouse admits that he does not want to become Louisa's "persecutor," and he is touched,
Dickens tells us, "in the cavity where his heart
should have been." With this phrase you'll understand the irony of Harthouse's name!

Sissy asks him to leave town as the only repar-
ation he can make to Louisa. Harthouse protests
that he has political business in Coketown that
must be attended to, but Sissy is unmoved. His
leaving is the only way to compensate for the
damage he has done. Harthouse is powerless in
the face of Sissy's powerful moral character. He
asks her to keep this business a secret and agrees
to leave town.

Do you find Harthouse's decision to leave town
believable? Do you think he would give up
Louisa without a fight? Some readers feel that he
is too easily intimidated by Sissy, while others
point to his history of easy boredom to suggest
that he is not strongly committed to anything.
Most readers agree, however, that for the purposes of the novel (particularly if you see it as an
allegory) it is important for Harthouse to be
confronted by Sissy, who represents the moral
strength he lacks. The pang he feels in the place
where his heart should be suggests that even
Harthouse is moved by the wisdom of the heart
that Sissy embodies.

Heading out of town on a railway carriage, Harthouse feels uncomfortable at having failed and
looking ridiculous to other men of his type. What
other moral men might feel—relief at having es-
caped before lives were seriously damaged—does
not faze him at all.

CHAPTER III

Mrs. Sparsit, stricken by a terrible cold as a result of her spying on Louisa, searches for Bounderby. When she finds him she spills her news about Louisa—and dramatically faints! Bounderby revives her as best he can, then takes her, "more dead than alive," on a train into Coketown. Ushering her into Gradgrind's house, Bounderby confronts Gradgrind and tells him that Mrs. Sparsit has something shocking to tell him about Harthouse and Louisa. Gradgrind says that he knows what went on between the pair and that the girl is now under his own roof, where she has come for protection.

Bounderby is outraged at Mrs. Sparsit for putting him in such an embarrassing position. He demands an apology, but when she claims to be too weak to offer one, he orders her back to her home.

Alone with Gradgrind, Bounderby insists he has not received due respect or proper treatment from Louisa. Gradgrind suggests that they both might have misunderstood her, that perhaps certain areas of her education have been badly handled. Perhaps it would be best, he tells Bounderby, that Louisa stay at the Gradgrind home for a time.

Bounderby assumes that Louisa is merely spoiled. If there's any incompatibility between them, he fumes, it comes from Louisa's lack of appreciation for her husband!

Gradgrind moves to end the conversation before either of them says something regrettable. But Bounderby insists that Louisa return to his house by noon tomorrow. If she doesn't, he'll assume she wishes to return to being Louisa Gradgrind, and he'll turn over responsibility for her to her father. Gradgrind advises caution, but Bounderby is firm.

By five minutes past noon the next day, Bounderby sends Louisa's possessions to the Gradgrind house and he resumes his bachelor life.

NOTE: Dickens never brings up the specific question of divorce between Louisa and Bounderby. It is implied that a divorce never takes place. Is there a legal complication or a moral objection on the part of husband or wife? The answer is never given.

CHAPTER IV

Bounderby buries his unhappiness in his work. The robbery is his chief source of concern, and he offers a reward for Stephen's arrest.

The workers are abuzz when the reward notice is posted all over town. Slackbridge, the union organizer, uses the poster at a meeting to show what happens to a man who betrays the union.

The same evening, Bounderby, Tom, and Rachael come to visit Louisa. Cold and distant, Bounderby faces Louisa for the first time since they separated. Rachael has been claiming certain things that Tom refuses to comment on.

Rachael reminds Louisa of the evening that she and her brother visited Stephen's room. As Rachael speaks, Tom stays quietly in the background, occasionally coughing to signal Louisa not to say anything that might incriminate him.

Louisa confirms Rachael's words. Tom insists that he could not say anything to Bounderby because he had promised Louisa not to—which is true. Besides, he adds, Louisa can tell the story so much better.

When Rachael read the reward poster, she wrote to Stephen to urge him to come home within two days to clear his name. Bounderby won't believe her; the mails have been watched, and no letters have left Coketown addressed to Stephen Blackpool. Rachael explains that Stephen is living under an assumed name—the only way he can get work. For Bounderby, this only proves the man's guilt.

Rachael refuses to reveal where Stephen is, certain that he will come back on his own. She leaves with Sissy's promise to visit her the next night. Gradgrind, who has remained silent the entire time, wonders who *is* guilty if Stephen is not. And where is the criminal?

Two days go by with no word from Stephen. More time passes, and Rachael finally goes to the bank to give Bounderby Stephen's last address. Messengers are sent to the place, but Stephen has already left.

Tom becomes increasingly nervous and upset. As another week passes, the town begins to wonder if Rachael's letter to Stephen was sent as a warning to escape.

CHAPTER V

Sissy goes to Rachael's room every night to comfort her. Most of the Coketown citizens are bored with the topic and assume Stephen is guilty. But Rachael's faith remains strong, helped by Sissy's support.

Rachael begins to wonder if there is someone in Coketown who would be proven guilty by Stephen's return. If so, could Stephen have been murdered on his way back?

One evening as Rachael is walking Sissy home, they pass the Bounderby house. There Mrs. Sparsit is getting out of a carriage, and she insists that the two women come into the house with her. Mrs. Sparsit has found Mrs. Pegler, the woman suspected of being Stephen's accomplice!

Mrs. Sparsit drags the protesting Mrs. Pegler into the house. Bounderby is with Gradgrind and Tom, and instead of being thrilled at Mrs. Sparsit's valiant efforts to find Mrs. Pegler, he condemns Mrs. Sparsit for interfering. As for Mrs. Pegler, she beams and addresses Bounderby as "My darling boy!"

NOTE: You've probably guessed long ago that Mrs. Pegler is Bounderby's mother. The fact that his humiliation happens in front of Gradgrind, Tom, Sissy, Rachael, and Mrs. Sparsit—and an audience of neighbors!—is one of the minor plot conveniences that many find a bit hard to believe.

Mrs. Pegler swears to Bounderby that she told no one he was her son. She agreed to go with Mrs. Sparsit only when the other woman threatened to call the police.

Gradgrind wonders how Mrs. Pegler has the nerve to claim Bounderby as her son after her cruel treatment of him as a boy. Mrs. Pegler is aston-ished. Bounderby was given every opportunity their poor family could afford, she says. The grand-mother who supposedly raised him had actually died before he was born, and Bounderby was ap-prenticed to a kind master at the age of eight. For many years he has paid his mother a pension to stay out of his life. Her yearly visits to Coketown were her only opportunity to see him—and then only from a distance.

A highly embarrassed Bounderby refuses to dis-cuss any family business with those present. What can he say now that he's revealed as a fraud? And imagine Mrs. Sparsit's feelings! She brought Mrs. Pegler hoping to atone for her failed attempts to prove that Louisa was an adulteress.

NOTE: Dickens's reference to Mrs. Sparsit in the Slough of Despond is taken from John Bunyan's *Pilgrim's Progress* (1678). The Slough of Despond is an allegorical symbol for the most intense state of despair.

Later, Gradgrind points out that Mrs. Pegler's innocence is a good sign for Stephen. But Louisa worries that Tom is the person who would benefit if Stephen never returned. Sissy shares the sus-picion, but the two women never discuss the mat-ter. And the doubt still lingers: if Stephen *is* in-nocent, where is he?

CHAPTER VI

On a lovely Sunday morning, Sissy and Rachael take a walk in the woods. The pollution of Coketown is so intense that they must take a train several miles out of town to find clean air.

Along the path, Sissy spots a rotten piece of fence that looks recently broken. Investigating it further, they find footprints, and near the footprints, a hat with Stephen Blackpool's name on it.

Venturing cautiously, afraid of what they might find, they come upon the open pit of an abandoned mine. Certain that Stephen is there, Rachael becomes hysterical. First Sissy and then Rachael call into the mine several times, but there is no answer. In desperation the two women separate and look for help.

Soon they have roused nearby villagers, who spread the word that someone has fallen down the Old Hell Shaft. A message is sent to Louisa, and the villagers gather equipment to pull Stephen out of the pit, if he is down there.

The common thought is that there is little hope that whoever is in the pit has survived. By the time a device for hoisting the body is erected, Gradgrind, Tom, Louisa, and Bounderby have arrived from town.

One man descends into the pit and comes out minutes later with the news that Stephen is alive, but badly hurt. Stephen has told his rescuer that he fell on the way to Bounderby's after dark. He's been lying there for several days, kept alive by scraps of food in his pocket.

After a painful wait, Stephen is finally pulled from the shaft, weak and near death. Barely able to speak, he tells Rachael that the pit that has caused his death had killed thousands when it was in use, and now it kills again. It's all "a muddle," he says. If it weren't, none of this would have happened. Stephen calls Rachael's attention to a star above them, one that gave him hope as he was lying in the pit. It made him think of Rachael, and it has helped him to clear away some of the muddle.

The presence of the star suggests that there may be peace in heaven for Stephen, far more than he ever had on earth.

Stephen then asks Gradgrind to clear his name, suggesting that he question Tom how that might be done. Some of the villagers carry Stephen out of the field, and he asks to hold Rachael's hand. As they move slowly along, the rescue party becomes a funeral procession. Stephen is dead.

NOTE: With his death, Stephen's martyrdom is complete. It is not accidental that he dies in an abandoned mine, one used to provide the coal for the steam engines that are so much a part of Coketown. Some would say that the symbolism is too obvious, that it is another example of Dickens's use of allegory overwhelming the credibility of the story. If you agree, you might find Stephen's death less than moving. If you don't, you might feel as saddened as many of Dickens's contemporaries were.

CHAPTER VII

Tom has slipped away from the crowd surrounding Stephen. When Gradgrind returns home, he sends for his son, but Bounderby reports that the boy has disappeared.

Gradgrind promises Bounderby that he will soon prove Stephen's innocence, then locks himself in his office, refusing company or food. He emerges the next morning looking older, but somehow is a "wiser" and "better" man.

Feeling certain that Tom robbed the bank, Louisa and Gradgrind wonder how to find him. It is Sissy who provides the answer. At the site of Stephen's accident, she whispered in Tom's ear a suggestion that he escape to Sleary's circus and told him how to find it. She promised that Sleary would hide him until she arrived. From there Tom could be sent to a safe, distant place.

Sissy and Louisa travel to the circus together, with Gradgrind using a different route to avoid Bounderby's suspicions. The two women journey all night, arriving in time to sit through the show as they await Sleary.

Sleary, Sissy, and the performers have a joyful reunion. Louisa asks about Tom, and Sleary takes her and Sissy to a peephole to watch one of the acts in progress. Among the characters performing are two servants in black makeup. One of them is Tom. Sleary tells the visitors to return with Gradgrind after the show.

Hours later, Sleary ushers Gradgrind, Louisa, and Sissy into the tent. Gradgrind sits on a clown chair. On a back bench, still in a ridiculous costume and wearing black makeup, sits Tom, as sullen as ever.

Dickens milks the scene for every last bit of irony. Tom is discovered in the very place we met him—at Sleary's Horse-riding. But now he is a lowly performer, wearing silly clothes and comic makeup. The dignified Gradgrind sits ludicrously in a clown's chair. The troupe that he once looked on with disapproval and condescension has saved his son from arrest. Unlike the coincidence of Stephen falling into a coal mine, this scene is applauded by most readers as both plausible and moving. Why do you think many find it to be so effective?

Gradgrind is saddened that his "model" son should be brought to this. Tom admits with typical bad temper to stealing the money. But he doesn't think his father should be surprised. Don't the percentages suggest that a certain number of people in trustworthy positions will turn out to be dishonest?

Tom is throwing into his father's face all that he has been taught by him. How do you feel about Gradgrind here? Is he getting what he deserves? Or have you come to see him as less evil and more misguided?

Gradgrind tells Tom that he must be sent out of the country. Tom agrees; he can't be more unhappy than he is right now. Sleary has a plan to sneak him out of town disguised as a carter (a country farmhand).

When Louisa tries to embrace him, Tom turns on her, accusing her of betraying him when he needed her most. Louisa is devastated.

Just as Tom is about to escape, the dreadful Bitzer appears! He's tracked them down, refusing to be outsmarted by circus people. He grabs Tom by the collar and won't let him go.

CHAPTER VIII

Gradgrind pleads with Bitzer. Doesn't the young man have a heart? Bitzer replies like the prize student he was in school: "The circulation, sir, couldn't be carried on without one." Again Gradgrind's careful theories backfire in his face.

Bitzer plans to take Tom back to Bounderby in hopes of being promoted to Tom's old job. Gradgrind offers Bitzer money, but the greedy one has already calculated that he can make more money from the promotion.

Gradgrind makes one more plea for Bitzer's mercy, reminding him of all the hard work lavished on him in Gradgrind's school. Bitzer is unmoved. The school was paid for, he explains, and it was a bargain. But the school is over and he owes no more. His reply is vintage Gradgrind philosophy!

Sleary offers to drive Tom and Bitzer to the railway station, but the circus owner has a trick up his sleeve to help Tom escape. The next morning Sleary reports that his plan has worked. Tom is on a ship bound for another country.

Gradgrind gives what little reward Sleary will accept for his troupe. Sleary asks to talk to him. Some months ago, Sissy's father's dog, Merrylegs, returned to the company, lame and almost blind. Sleary knows that Mr. Jupe is dead, because the dog would never leave its master. He suggests that Sissy not be told, for it would only break her heart.

The return of the dog has shown Sleary once again that there *is* love in the world, not just self-interest, and that the ways of love are as mysterious as those of a dog.

Sleary has some parting advice for Gradgrind. He asks him not to be too hard on vagabonds such as they. He repeats the advice he gave in Book the First, Chapter 6: people need to be amused as much as they need to learn or to work. Make the best of things, Sleary suggests, not the worst.

CHAPTER IX

Bounderby is furious with Mrs. Sparsit for having accidentally brought his past to life by returning Mrs. Pegler to Coketown. He decides to fire her as the most damaging punishment. Suggesting she go to her wealthy relation, Lady Scadgers, Bounderby sends Mrs. Sparsit on her way. Mrs. Sparsit returns insult for insult. She replies that nothing a "noodle" says or does should ever surprise—"noodles" can only "inspire contempt." And with that she sweeps out of the room and out of Bounderby's life.

Bounderby and Mrs. Sparsit, for all of his money and her breeding, can't keep their final argument on a polite tone. They are reduced to insults and name-calling. Bounderby's plan to wound Mrs. Sparsit backfires when he discovers she's hated him for a long time.

NOTE: Gradgrind and Bounderby Have you noticed a difference in the way Gradgrind and Bounderby are each handled in the novel? At first, because they are friends, it may seem that Bounderby and Gradgrind are very much alike. But you have seen how a rude awakening has changed Gradgrind for the better. He is a wiser man for his experiences. There is no such wisdom for Bounderby. He is the same pompous, greedy humbug he was at the very first. Readers have pointed out that Bounderby and Gradgrind seem to come from two different modes of writing. Bounderby is a character from comic fiction, like the exaggerated cartoons Dickens created for *The Pickwick Papers*. He is always the same and never grows as a human being. (The same might be said of Mrs. Sparsit.) Gradgrind, on the other hand, is more fully drawn, closer to the realistic techniques of Dickens's later novels. That they inhabit the same book suggests to some that Dickens is inconsistent in his characterizations. Others delight in the fact that the universe of a Dickens novel can embrace both types successfully.

The rest of the novel looks to the future. Mrs. Sparsit will lead a bickering, penny-pinching life with Lady Scadgers. Only Sissy—the wisdom of the heart from the very first—seems completely fulfilled. As for the citizens of Coketown, no magic formula cleans the air or the water or the skies; no solution is found for the greed of the employers or the manipulation of the union. Life is much as it was when the novel began. What some of the characters learn about themselves is not enough to make a difference in the town's miserable existence. The ending is one of the reasons *Hard Times* is considered by many to be Dickens's harshest, most bitter novel.

A STEP BEYOND

Tests and Answers
TESTS

Test 1

1. Stephen's promise not to join the union _____
   A. is made in front of several witnesses
   B. is never fully explained in the novel
   C. was one made by many factory workers

2. Mr. Jupe's dog Merrylegs represents _____
   A. love and loyalty that defies understanding
   B. the sick and the aged
   C. animal instinct

3. Stephen's dream _____
   A. convinces him to try to kill his wife
   B. foreshadows his own death
   C. takes place while he is lying in the abandoned mine

4. Mrs. Pegler returns to Coketown each year _____ to
   A. haunt Gradgrind
   B. find out how Bounderby is doing
   C. take revenge on her son

5. Tom is eager to see Louisa marry Bounderby because _____

A. he knows how much she loves him
B. life will be easier for him
C. Gradgrind urges him to support the marriage

6. Sissy's father abandons her because he _____
   A. feels that she could manage on her own
   B. doesn't want her to see him age
   C. has an offer from another circus

7. Mrs. Sparsit's Staircase _____
   I. symbolizes Louisa's descent into adultery
   II. is an indication of Mrs. Sparsit's obsessive interest in Louisa
   III. leads to a secret room at the bank
       A. I and III only   B. I and II only
       C. II and III only

8. Bitzer shows himself to be a prize graduate _____
   of the Gradgrind school when he
   I. correctly defines a horse
   II. says that a heart is good for circulation
   III. refuses to take money from Gradgrind for Tom's release
       A. I and II only   B. I and III only
       C. I, II, and III

9. Stephen's phrase "It's a muddle" _____
   A. refers to Louisa's marriage
   B. describes his life in Coketown
   C. is repeated often by Bounderby

10. Louisa's calm exterior _____

    A. hides emotions that she rarely releases
    B. is inherited from her mother
    C. reminds Rachael of Stephen's wife's
       face

11. Compare the characters of Josiah Bounderby and Thomas Gradgrind, Sr.

12. What is the function of Sleary's "Horse-riding" in *Hard Times*?

13. Discuss the symbolism of the star seen by Stephen Blackpool?

14. Why is Sissy Jupe important to the novel?

15. In what ways is *Hard Times* an allegory?

Test 2

1. The workers of Coketown read   _____
    A. every newspaper account of Stephen
       Blackpool's death
    B. Bounderby's newspaper column
    C. more books of fiction than books of
       science

2. Harthouse comes to Coketown because he _____
    I. has been asked by the Gradgrind
      political party
    II. is bored
    III. met Louisa in London
        A. I only   B. I and II only
        C. II and III only

3. Dickens considers Coketown   _____
    A. a jungle
    B. superior to most factory towns
    C. to be improving every year

4. Rachael and Sissy fear that Stephen may be _____
in danger when
   A. Mrs. Pegler has a dream about him
   B. they find his hat in the country
   C. Bitzer acts suspiciously

5. Stephen leaves town _____
   A. because he can't find work in
      Coketown
   B. when he learns the bank has been
      robbed
   C. to search for his wife

6. Mrs. Sparsit is convinced that Louisa and _____
Harthouse are lovers
   A. when she sees them talking in the
      garden
   B. because she hears Louisa accept his
      proposal of marriage
   C. when Bounderby tells her of the letter
      he found

7. "People mutht be amuthed" is spoken by _____
   A. Slackbridge   B. Rachael
   C. Sleary

8. A "whelp" is _____
   I. the offspring of an animal
   II. Harthouse's nickname for Tom
   III. Mrs. Pegler's pet name for Bounderby
      A. I and III only   B. I and II only
      C. II and III only

9. A driving rainstorm creates tension in what _____
scene?

   A. Stephen's departure from Coketown
   B. Mrs. Sparsit's pursuit of Louisa
   C. Sissy's discovery of her father's departure

10. Sissy is kept from leaving the Gradgrind _____ household
   A. when Gradgrind locks her in her room
   B. by her hope that her father will return
   C. by her deep love for Mrs. Gradgrind

11. Readers often find Stephen unrealistic. Discuss.

12. Discuss the significance of the titles of the three books of *Hard Times:* "Sowing," "Reaping," "Garnering."

13. Explain the significance of "turtle soup and venison with a gold spoon."

14. Discuss how Louisa is identified with fire in the novel.

15. Discuss the relationship of Mrs. Sparsit and Bounderby.

ANSWERS

Test 1

1. B	**2.** A	**3.** B	**4.** B	**5.** B	**6.** B
7. B	**8.** C	**9.** B	**10.** A		

11. Dickens at first seems to suggest that Bounderby and Gradgrind come from the same mold. They are good friends, and they agree in theory on matters of education, politics, and the workers of Coketown. But as the novel unfolds, it becomes clear that the men are basically different. Bounderby is essentially a capitalist, concerned with his own greed at the expense of the factory workers. Gradgrind is a politician and philosopher who believes that his ideas are promoting "the greatest happiness for the greatest number." Trying to do good, Gradgrind has become blinded and oppressive, but his intentions are decent.

Gradgrind is capable of learning from his mistakes. Bounderby is not. When Gradgrind is made aware of Louisa's unhappiness, he undergoes a major change of attitude; he grows from the experience. When Bounderby is made aware of Louisa's misery, and when he is exposed as a liar and a fraud, he undergoes no change. He is as selfish and pompous as ever. In short, Gradgrind is a more rounded, complex character than Bounderby, who retains the same postures and prejudices from beginning to end.

12. The "Horse-riding" first represents all that is harmful and dangerous in the Bounderby/Gradgrind world. Because the circus exists only for the purposes of entertainment—"fancy"—it is seen as a threat to the pursuit of fact that Gradgrind regards as the basis of education. Tom and Louisa's interest in the troupe of performers suggests their eventual rebellion from the dictates of their father.

By the end of the novel, the "horse-riding" is seen as necessary to the well-being of the citizens of Coketown, as important as learning and work. People must be amused, says Sleary, and he speaks to man's need to escape from his world to the world of imagination. Citizens deprived of such escape end up emotionally repressed or possibly criminal, as evidenced by the characters of Louisa and Tom.

The horse-riding also serves a symbolic plot device. Tom, fleeing from the law, ends up in hiding there as a clown. And it is Sleary who provides him not only with a hiding place but with a means to escape from the country. The troupe that Gradgrind once treated with sneering disdain has saved his son from arrest. "Fancy" has, in one sense, become Gradgrind's salvation as well.

13. Stephen first sees the star as he's lying in the pit of the abandoned mine. He tells Rachael as he's dying that the star made him think of her and that it helped clear away some of the "muddle" from his mind. For Stephen, the "muddle" represents the whole confused tangle of his life—from his disastrous marriage to the unhappy plight of the working man. The star that brings some clarity to this "muddle" suggests both Rachael, who was the only bright light in his existence, and the heavenly rest that he will soon enjoy. As the villagers carry Stephen's body toward that star, we are told that it leads to "the god of the poor." Because Stephen symbolizes all of the oppressed workers that Dickens champions in this book, the star symbolizes the reward that Dickens feels waits for them at their death, a reward they would never enjoy in this life.

14. Sissy Jupe is the one character who is wholly good. Though at first she is scorned by Gradgrind and Bounderby for being a performer's daughter, and then is removed from school because she cannot learn the Gradgrind way, Sissy slowly exerts a moral force of goodness on many of the characters. After a period of time in the Gradgrind household, she makes her mark on the younger children and even on Mrs. Gradgrind, providing a "spirit" that even Gradgrind notices (but cannot identify). The "Wisdom of the Heart" that Sissy represents (and which Dickens implies is the true wisdom, superior to that of the head) is felt by Louisa, Rachael, and even Harthouse. Without her, the novel would have no standard by which to judge the other characters and their moral flaws. Of all the characters, only Sissy will go on to know the pleasures of a family. As a product of the world of "fancy" (the "horse-riding"), Sissy underscores the coldhearted and destructive influences of the world of fact.

15. In answering this question, you should first define "allegory." (An allegory is a story in which characters represent concepts or abstractions, usually to underline a moral principle.) Then you should choose the characters you feel are most allegorical and talk about what they represent. For example, Gradgrind represents the philosophy of Utilitarianism, a leading political movement that believes in "the greatest happiness for the greatest number." Bounderby stands for the greed and insensitivity of capitalism, more concerned with profit than with the welfare of his workers. Stephen is the "martyred" working man, oppressed and exploited by both management and the organizers and leaders of the union. Mrs. Sparsit and Harthouse stand for the aristocracy: she clings to past snobbery and false superiority; he is bored, cynical, rootless, and amoral. Through Sleary's circus we see the kindhearted and generous vagabonds who bring pleasure through entertainment and provide "fancy" to a starving populace fed only on fact. And Sissy Jupe, the product of that environment, is a symbol of moral good that eventually conquers much of what is self-interested and harmful in the world.

Test 2
1. C   **2.** B   **3.** A   **4.** B   **5.** A   **6.** A
7. C   **8.** B   **9.** B   **10.** B

11. Stephen is considered unrealistic for two basic reasons. First, some readers charge that he has been burdened with an unbelievable number of obstacles—a drunken wife, his inability to get a divorce, his rejection by both the union and Bounderby, his implication in the bank robbery—followed by his eventual accidental death in the pit of an abandoned mine. It is suggested that, by creating a character so oppressed by circumstance, Dickens strains the reader's credibility and weakens the social criticism implied by the character.

Second, Stephen is made the spokesperson for the factory worker, particularly in two scenes in Bounderby's house. His speeches are often considered unrealistic because they seem less like the words of a typical factory worker and more like Dickens's own sentiments. It is here, some charge, that Dickens the reformer overwhelms Dickens the writer of social realism.

12. "Sowing" suggests the seeds planted by the Bounderby/Gradgrind philosophy, particularly as seen through Louisa and Tom. They are raised as products of this strict philosophy and grow according to its dictates. By the end of the first book, Gradgrind has no reason to feel that his "crop" will be anything but successful: Louisa is about to make a profitable marriage, and Tom will begin a job at the bank. Stephen, too, is the product of this sowing. In "Reaping," however, this harvest reveals itself to be a bitter one. Louisa's marriage is unhappy, and she nearly runs off with another man. Tom turns out to be a gambler, liar, and thief, and Gradgrind's philosophy brutally explodes in his own face. Stephen is rejected by his fellow workers and loses his job. In "Garnering," the results of the harvest are gathered up and taken home. Gradgrind experiences the pain of an ungrateful and unrepentant son. Louisa faces a future without a family of her own. Tom must leave the country. And Stephen is dead.

All three titles have Biblical implications. The first two suggest the text, "Whatsoever a man soweth, that shall he also reap" (Galatians 6:7). "Garnering" suggests the story of Ruth, who garnered corn in the fields of Boaz.

13. This is the phrase used often by Bounderby to signify what he believes to be the typical request of a Coketown factory worker. Such an opinion typifies Bounderby's awesome insensitivity to his worker's needs. He feels they are lazy, enjoy easy jobs, spend too much time at play, and live in healthful surroundings. Dickens goes to great pains in the novel to suggest how wrong Bounderby is, and how he is typical of what is wrong with a society that permits such stupidity and greed to prevail.

14. When we first see Louisa, she is compared to "a fire with nothing to burn," suggesting her "starved imagination" that has only fed on the thin diet of facts her father has given her. Later, Louisa is seen gazing into the fire as her marriage to Bounderby seems more and more inevitable. The fading embers are compared to her own concept of her future as hopeless and short. Most importantly, she refers to fire when Gradgrind tells her of Bounderby's proposal. Louisa's response is to mention the chimneys of Coketown, which seem to spew only languid and monotonous smoke until suddenly— a burst of flame! Louisa refers to her own passion for life that lurks beneath her cool exterior, hoping that her father will understand that a marriage to Bounderby will never unleash those passions. But Gradgrind is too insensitive to his daughter's hidden meaning, and the "burst of flame" (heralded by lightning) comes after her marriage and through her friendship with Harthouse.

15. Mrs. Sparsit is Bounderby's housekeeper, and at the beginning of the novel, she seems content with her role as Bounderby's chief source of pride. Because of her aristocratic heritage, Bounderby loves to point to her as an example of how far he has come in the world. Mrs. Sparsit is only too happy to listen to his praise. When Bounderby marries Louisa, the relationship between him and Mrs. Sparsit becomes more ambiguous. She is clearly jealous of Louisa, but whether she wants to be Mrs. Bounderby or simply his housekeeper again is uncertain. She *is* obsessed with proving Louisa to be an adulteress, but at times it seems that she wants to prove to Bounderby that he's the "noodle" she calls him behind his back. Their "friendship" ends when she unwittingly reveals him as a fraud by bringing Mrs. Pegler out in the open. Mrs. Sparsit's contempt for him is evident when he fires her from his employ, but whether the contempt is borne of love or hatred is never fully explained.

Term Paper Ideas and other Topics for Writing

The Novel

1. What role did the Industrial Revolution play in the writing of *Hard Times*?

2. How does the weekly serial form affect the structure of the novel?

3. In what ways can *Hard Times* be considered a bitter novel? A hopeful novel?

4. How does the social criticism of the novel compare with that of *Bleak House*? Of *Little Dorrit*?

5. In Chapter 4 of Book the Second, the narrator comments, "Private feeling must yield to the common cause." Explain this in terms of the novel's events and relate it to a current situation.

Characters

1. Compare and contrast Bounderby and Gradgrind.

2. In what ways can Stephen be considered a martyr?

3. Who is the main character of *Hard Times*? Defend your choice.

4. How are the various levels of society represented by the characters?

5. Comment on the significance of Louisa's remark to her father, "You have been so careful of me that I never had a child's heart."

6. What role does Sissy Jupe play in the novel?

7. Compare the characterization of Sleary and his troupe with the Crummles acting company of *Nicholas Nickleby.*

8. How is Gradgrind educated in the course of the novel?

9. How does Mrs. Gradgrind function in the novel?

10. Is Harthouse a round or a flat character? Explain.

11. How are Sissy and Bitzer compared early in the novel? Why? Is the comparison developed?

12. How is the parent/child relationship handled in the novel? Pay special attention to the Gradgrinds, the Jupes, and Bounderby and Mrs. Pegler.

13. Describe the effect Sissy Jupe has on the lives of three of the major characters.

14. In what ways is Mr. Jupe's presence felt throughout the novel? How does he affect one of the story's chief morals?

15. Chart the progress of Mrs. Sparsit's relationship with Bounderby.

16. Why is Bounderby called "the Bully of Humility"?

17. In what ways is Stephen a realistic character? In what ways is he not?

18. Compare M'Choakumchild's school and its theory of education to that of Wackford Squeers's in *Nicholas Nickleby* or to some other novel which uses this topic.

19. In what ways does Bitzer prove himself to be the prize Gradgrind pupil?

20. How does Dickens use names to signify his characters' traits?

21. How does the presence of Mrs. Pegler add suspense to the novel?

22. Looking at Dickens's life, find out which of the characters in *Hard Times* have autobiographical overtones.

Literary Topics

1. How is irony used in the death of Stephen Blackpool?

2. Discuss the ways in which Coketown is seen metaphorically as a jungle.

3. How is coincidence used in the novel? Is it beneficial or harmful to the realism of the book?

4. How does Dickens use comedy in the novel? Cite at least five examples.

5. In what way does Christianity affect the tone of the novel? What Christian symbols are used?

6. In what ways is *Hard Times* a satire? Explain.

7. How are colors used as symbols in the characters of Sissy and Bitzer?

8. Discuss the symbolism of the circus and how it relates to the novel as a whole.

Miscellaneous

1. Research the efforts to organize unions in the United States in the early part of the twentieth century. How are they similar to those described in *Hard Times?* How are they different?

2. In what ways does the novel speak to us today? Are any of the issues presented by Dickens still with us? Which ones?

Further Reading

CRITICAL WORKS

Andrews, Malcolm. *Dickens on England and the English.* New York: Harper and Row, 1979. Dickens as social observer and critic.

Collins, Philip. *Dickens and Education.* New York: St. Martin's, 1963. The historical basis for the Gradgrind school and others in Dickens's works.

Collins, Philip, ed. *Dickens: The Critical Heritage.* London: Routledge and Kegan Paul, 1971. A collection of critical essays on Dickens, with emphasis on the nineteenth century.

Donovan, Frank. *Dickens and Youth.* New York: Dodd, Mead, 1969. An examination of Dickens's treatment of children.

Hobsbaum, Philip. "Hard Times." *A Reader's Guide to Charles Dickens.* New York: Farrar, Straus, and Giroux, 1972, pp. 173–87.

Holloway, John. "Hard Times." *Dickens and the Twentieth Century.* Edited by John Gross and Gabriel Pearson. London: Routledge and Kegan Paul, 1962, pp. 165–74.

Johnson, Edgar. *Charles Dickens: His Tragedy and Triumph.* New York: Viking, 1977. A revised abridgment of the definitive two-volume biography.

Leavis, F. R. "Hard Times: An Analytic Note." In *The Great Tradition.* New York: New York University Press, 1964. This essay, written in 1950, did a great deal to boost the novel's reputation.

Lucas, John. *The Melancholy Man: A Study of Dickens' Novels.* London: Methuen, 1970.

MacKenzie, Norman, and Jeanne MacKenzie. *Dickens: A Life.* New York: Oxford University Press, 1979. One of the best of the recent Dickens's biographies.

Shaw, George Bernard. "Introduction to *Hard Times*."
In *Dickens: The Critical Heritage*. Edited by Philip
Collins. London: Routledge and Kegan Paul, 1971,
pp. 335–39.

Slater, Michael, ed. *Dickens 1970*. New York: Stein and
Day, 1970. A collection of critical essays on the cen-
tenary of Dickens's death.

Thurley, Geoffrey. *The Dickens Myth*. New York: St. Martin's, 1976.

Vogel, Jane. *Allegory in Dickens*. University: University
of Alabama Press, 1977. A detailed examination of the
uses of allegory in *Hard Times* and other works.

Wilson, Angus. *The World of Charles Dickens*. New York:
Viking, 1970. A biography handsomely illustrated with
contemporary paintings and etchings.

AUTHOR'S OTHER WORKS

1836	*Sketches by Boz*
1836–37	*The Pickwick Papers*
1837–38	*Oliver Twist*
1838–39	*Nicholas Nickleby*
1840–41	*The Old Curiosity Shop*
1841	*Barnaby Rudge*
1842	*American Notes*
1843–44	*Martin Chuzzlewit*
1843	*A Christmas Carol*
1844	*The Chimes*
1845	*The Cricket on the Hearth*
1846–48	*Dombey and Son*
1849–50	*David Copperfield*
1852–53	*Bleak House*
1855–57	*Little Dorrit*
1859	*A Tale of Two Cities*
1860–61	*Great Expectations*

Glossary

Adam Smith   One of Thomas Gradgrind's younger sons, named after the British economist whose doctrine of *laissez-faire* Dickens felt resulted in many of the abuses of the Industrial Revolution.

Alderny   A breed of dairy cattle.

Beadle   In the Anglican church, a parish official who keeps order during the services, waits on the clergyman, etc.

Bluebeard   A fictional character known for having several wives, all of whom he murdered.

Brutus   A Roman politician; one of the men who assassinated Julius Caesar.

Carter   A country bumpkin; Tom Gradgrind's disguise when he attempts to flee the country.

Centaur   A mythical beast with the head, trunk, and arms of a man and the body and legs of a horse.

Chandler   Someone who sells trinkets door-to-door; also, one who makes candles.

Cocker, Edwin   Famous British mathematician whose accuracy was so respected that the phrase "according to Cocker" came to mean "according to fact."

Doctors Commons   The law courts that specialized in divorce cases in nineteenth-century England.

Equestrian   Pertaining to horses or horsemanship.

Fairy palaces   Dickens's ironic name for the Coketown factories, given because they resemble glittering palaces when seen from a speeding train.

Gaming   Gambling.

Gorgon   A hideous woman. In Greek mythology, a Gorgon was a woman with serpents growing from her head.

Graces   Three goddesses associated with the enjoyment of life.

"Hands"   Collective name for Coketown factory employees.

Hey-go-mad   Very excited.

Horse-riding   A traveling circus specializing in horse acts.

House of Commons   The lower house of British Parliament, whose representatives are elected.

House of Lords   The upper, nonelective House of Parliament.

Light porter   Messenger; Bitzer's job at Bounderby's bank.

Lord Chesterfield   Philip Dormer Stanhope, the fourth earl of Chesterfield (1694–1773); famous for his letters to his son, which are full of advice about education, breeding, and morals.

Lord Harry   The devil.

Malthus   British mathematician whose theories on population Dickens found objectionable and dangerous; also, the name given to one of Gradgrind's younger sons.

Merrylegs   Mr. Jupe's dog, seen as a symbol of eternal loyalty.

Misanthrope   A person who hates mankind.

Morgiana   Ali Baba's servant in the *Arabian Nights* tales; her techniques are compared to those of M'Choakumchild.

Morris   To run away.

Ogre   A monster in fairy tales and fables, usually represented as a hideous giant.

Old Hell Shaft   The name of the abandoned mine shaft into which Stephen Blackpool falls.

Parliamentary   A train that provided the cheapest way

of travel; the means Mrs. Pegler uses to get from her home to Coketown.

Pegasus   A mythical flying horse.

Physic   A medicine that purges; a laxative.

Play old Gooseberry   To play havoc; said of Mrs. Blackpool.

Portico   A structure consisting of a roof supported by columns, usually attached to a building as a porch.

Postilion   A person who rides the horse on the left of the leading pair when four or more horses are used to draw a carriage.

Professor Owen   Sir Richard Owen, a well-known expert on comparative anatomy.

Public house   A tavern with rooms for renting.

Pugilist   A person who fights with his fists, usually professionally.

Robinson Crusoe   Hero of Daniel Defoe's famous novel, written in 1719; tells of a shipwrecked man who creates his own civilization on a deserted island.

Sent to Coventry   Shunned, rejected; said of Stephen Blackpool when he refuses to join the union.

Slough of Despond   An allegorical state of deep despair, from John Bunyan's *Pilgrim's Progress* (1678).

Spartan   Of or pertaining to the people of Sparta, a city of ancient Greece; Spartans were known for their discipline and bravery in the face of danger.

Stone Lodge   The Gradgrind family home.

Stroller   An itinerant performer.

Sweetbreads   The pancreas of a calf or lamb, considered a delicacy to eat.

Tower of Babel   A tower erected in the ancient city of Babel whose purpose was to reach God; the result was a confusion of languages.

Venus   Roman goddess of love and beauty.

Viands   An article of food, usually one considered a delicacy.

Victuals   Food supplies; provisions.

Whelp   The offspring of an animal; Dickens's term for Tom Gradgrind, Jr.

Windlass   A device used for hoisting; usually having a horizontal drum on which a rope attached to the load is wound.

The Critics

The Novel

Hard Times will stand up to a critical reading far better than any earlier novel of Dickens, *Bleak House* alone excepted. It portrays figures as remarkable for their individuality as any in the whole of Dickens, but, for the most part, they serve the considerations of Theme. And the Theme is one capable of engaging serious attention. For Dickens has made a highly serious claim. It is tripartite in character: that the paranoid temperament fosters a paranoid creed. Utilitarianism, and that this creed extends itself in practice into the irresponsible development of Industry. It is not Industry per se that Dickens is fighting; rather laissez-faire, which polluted the atmosphere, allowed open mine-shafts to fester, employed or starved workers according to the market without any sense of human need or potential. Not industry alone is in question, but the philosophy operating behind it. "Your sister's training has been pursued according to the system" says the broken Gradgrind; and it is true. *Hard Times,* then, is Dickens's attack upon the System by which the claims of individual human beings are trampled in a general mêlée. Society itself cannot survive under such circumstances. The answers of *Hard Times* may be invalid; the questions it propounds are still with us. It is the most flawed of Dickens's classics, possibly, but it is still a classic.

> —*Philip Hobsbaum,*
> A Reader's Guide to Charles
> Dickens, *1972*

[Hard Times] seems to me an unsuccessful novel, and for fairly obvious reasons. It has a bleakly deterministic view of the hopelessness of the human situation, and I think it is a sort of thesis-novel. Dickens marks out his enemies, Gradgrind and Bounderby, and he makes of them mere cyphers, predictable, hateful and easily condemned. But between them they represent a way of life which is meant to be powerful enough to squeeze out all hope for human decency. At the end of the novel, the circus-owner Sleary remarks to Gradgrind that

> people mutht be amused. They can't be alwayth a learning nor yet they can't be always a working, they ain't made for it. You *mutht* have us, Thquire.

Slearly undoubtedly is seen as embodying the novel's positive values; but his remark is feebly prescriptive. The chance of "fun" is infinitely remote from the lives of the Coketowners. And in terms of what the novel proposes, it follows that the people of Coketown are as good as dead.

—*John Lucas*,
The Melancholy Man, *1970*

In fact, if what is best in this novel is reviewed generally, it cannot but suggest reflections which extend beyond itself. For the passages in *Hard Times* where Dickens most shows his genius, is most freely himself, are not those where he is most engaged with his moral fable or intent (if we think, mistakenly, that he is so at all) on what Dr. Leavis called "the confutation of Utilitarianism by life." Rather, they appear when he comes near to being least engrossed with such things; when he is the Dickens who appears throughout the novels: the master of dialogue that, even through its stylization, crackles with life, perception, and sharpness, the master of drama in spectacle and setting and action.

—*John Holloway, "Hard Times,"*
Dickens and the Twentieth
Century, *1962*

Dickens and Trade Unions

There is, however, one real failure in the book. Slackbridge, the trade union organizer, is a mere figment of the middle-class imagination. No such man would be listened to by a meeting of English factory hands. Not that such meetings are less susceptible to humbug than meetings of any other class.

Not that trade union organizers, worn out by the terribly wearisome and trying work of going from place to place repeating the same commonplaces and trying to "stoke up" meetings to enthusiasm with them, are less apt than other politicians to end as windbags, and sometimes to depend on stimulants to pull them through their work. Not, in short, that the trade union platform is any less humbug-ridden than the platforms of our more highly placed political parties. But even at their worst trade union organizers are not a bit like Slackbridge. . . . Dickens knew certain classes of working folk very well: domestic servants, village artisans, and employees of petty tradesmen, for example. But of the segregated factory populations of our purely industrial towns he knew no more than an observant professional man can pick up on a flying visit to Manchester.

> —*George Bernard Shaw,*
> *"Introduction to 'Hard Times,' "*
> *(1912), in* Dickens: The Critical
> Heritage, *1971*

The Ending of Hard Times

It is the only conclusion in all Dickens that allows only the reserved "happy ending" of peace, of passion spent, of the end of disaster. It has no damaging bright glow of a future happiness for Louisa. Sissy's happy ending is not damaging, both because she has never been an actively, only a symbolically, prominent character; also because her happy marriage is brought in to emphasize Louisa's lack of glow. For once, even the children on the last page are tolerable.

There is a formality and solemnity in the language, and its quiet and reserve, . . . *a vox humana* with a difference, not too deep, shrill or ecstatic, and a turning away from grand climax. The moral suggestiveness is optimistic, but not only does the quieter language underline the mere spectator's solace that remains for Louisa, but also points two ways for the Dear reader. Though the last sentence speaks for the better way, it does so in the unradiant imagery of death, with no heavenly sunset glow but gray ashes, just right for Coketown. Coketown can be remembered in the last lines of *Hard Times* as the slums are not at the end of *Oliver Twist* or *Bleak House*, and this is right, since the human discovery has not cancelled out the world of Coketown.

—*Barbara Hardy, "The Complexity of Dickens" (1970), in* Dickens 1970

Stephen Blackpool

Blackpool himself is a further experiment in the direction of the fully achieved emblematicism of *A Tale of Two Cities*. In other words, he stands for a situation, a class, a predicament, without having to exist for us in quite the same way as Louisa or Sissy exist for us. We must avoid any temptation to condemn him as unreal, and recognize a perfectly valid literary mode. Dickens is doing something difficult and unprecedented here; he is creating a character real by the standards of Victorian realism, but capable of functioning as a symbolic, almost an abstract term in an argument.

—*Geoffrey Thurley,*
The Dickens Myth, *1976*

There are so many things that Dickens could have done with Stephen. More could have been made of the mine-shaft down which he falls: it ought to have been fenced in after it had been finished with, just as, when in use, its firedamp and propensity towards explosion could have been countered with protective devices: but at no point does Dickens erect it into a social indictment. More could have been made of Stephen's scanty income and conditions of labour at the mill. It is significant that never once in this industrial novel does Dickens show us the day to day life of men in a factory. It would take more than a visit to Preston or Hanley to dramatize this in any depth of detail; yet some such undertaking ought to have been at the heart of the book. Stephen, in fact, is not dramatized as archetypal

working man so much as a personification of a victim; not a social victim, either, but the victim of a
broken-down marriage.

—Philip Hobsbaum,
A Reader's Guide to Charles
Dickens, *1972*

NOTES

NOTES

NOTES

NOTES

NOTES